IN THE CRADLE OF UMBRA

AYHAN YAVUZ

Edited by Kathryn F. Galán, Wynnpix Productions
Cover Art by Ayhan Yavuz
Author's photos by Max Warren
www.Tresoea.com

*Disclaimer and Terms of Use: The author has striven to be as accurate and complete as possible
in the creation of this book but does not assume any responsibility for errors, omissions, or
contrary interpretation of the subject matter herein. Any perceived slights of specific persons,
peoples, or organizations are unintentional. Readers are cautioned to rely on their own
judgment about their individual circumstances and to act accordingly. This book is not
intended for use as a source of legal, business, accounting, or financial advice. All readers
are advised to seek services of competent professionals in the legal, business, accounting, and
finance fields.*

PRINT ISBN 978-1-5489-6155-8

This book is dedicated to my father, for embracing my free spirit; my mother for loving me unconditionally; my brothers, sisters, and everyone in my extended family for supporting my quest to find whatever I was looking for; my teachers with or without the title for their genuine interest in my learning; and my beautiful daughters, Olivia, Eden, and Ava, for shining their light on me when I needed the most.

There was a time when I considered not waking up from a sleep, when I almost believed it was not possible to climb out of the cradle of my umbra. That was when I realized there is light within the darkness.

CONTENTS

INTRODUCTION

WIKIPEDIA DEFINES the word *umbra* as the following:

> *The **umbra** (Latin for "shadow") is the innermost and darkest part of a shadow, where the light source is completely blocked by the occluding body. An observer in the umbra experiences a total eclipse.*

Probably just like you, I have found myself in a place where I thought I had been abandoned by the light and was trapped in the darkness. I still remember hearing the caring voices around me telling me, "*This, too, shall pass.*"

I can frankly say I wanted to believe them at the time of my suffering. Somehow, I wanted to believe that miracles do happen and that perhaps I had a guardian angel who would come to my rescue and lift me up above the swamp I had fallen into. But the truth is when you believe the darkness is here to stay, when it feels like your angel is no longer watching over you, when you don't know where you are, when you witness the burial of your dreams, and when you feel alone and forgotten, *I do not believe that the light is the first thing we see.* Instead, we repeat the same record of our victimhood as it plays the same song, mocking us and making fun of our failures.

Yes, I wrote this book for a reason. And no, it is not to satisfy my ego (at least not anymore). The word *umbra* perfectly describes what I was experiencing at the time I started writing this book.

Also, around the same time in my own suffering, I noticed how paralyzed most people looked during a long period of their suffering. It was like all the good things were right around them, the things that could help them escape the drama, but they had no energy to get out of the bed, to go out and feel the breeze in their faces, or to see the sunlight and smell the flowers. It was like they did not fit in. Everyone else's life seemed to be working perfectly, but their lives had been broken into pieces, and they were afraid to cut their hands on the shards of their shattered dreams. This place of paralysis had somehow become familiar to them. It provided them a resting place. That was when I decided I wanted to share my learning experience. The name of the book came to me, and I already had the story. This is exactly what it is to me. It is nothing but a story.

In the Cradle of Umbra is about a place and time: where and when we give up; where we are too afraid to get up; when we lose our hopes; where the light does not visit us and we start to consider ending everything for all time, starting with our lives.

It was a deceptive cradle for me, however. It almost rocked me into an eternal sleep from which I knew I had to wake up. The biggest mistake I made in my life was because of something I could not see at that time. I have realized since then that the suffering I went through was not only for me. It was like a tornado that sucked up everyone I loved and cared about.

I wanted to share my story, but I did not want this book be about me. Instead, I simply hope that my story can be a learning opportunity for those who someday might need it.

I suggest you take your time reading this book. It certainly should not be read as fiction. In fact, I believe it would be more beneficial to read one chapter at a time and let the material sink in. Questions will arise that will likely push you out of your comfort zone. There will also be metaphors that will encourage you to exercise your imagination.

There are fifty chapters in this book. Although each chapter focuses on something specific, at the end, you will notice they all are connected. In some chapters, there are stories, whereas in other, some scenarios are presented to you. Take your time when you read it, and be honest with yourself. Answer those questions with sincerity. **We all have stories: some have been shared, and some are still hidden in our own shadows.** Make a promise to yourself that you will always be committed to living the best version of your life, so you will not waste your precious life to fit into a mold created by the expectations of others. When life gets tough, keep reminding yourself to breathe in and then breathe out. Nothing is permanent. Life is not permanent. Neither should the suffering be.

1

MAGNETIC EMPTINESS

IN LIFE, THERE ARE more than four seasons. So there are also many unseen shades of color. Some people seem to be only just surviving during the season of winter, when their hearts feel paralyzed by the ice storms of life's unfairness. Some people appear to enjoy the never-ending sunshine in their loved ones' laughter. However, seasons never wait for anyone. They are never only for some of us. When the time comes, we can't help ourselves falling with autumn's leaves, finding warmth in the hearths of winter, welcoming the fairies of the creek in spring, and dancing on the warm beaches of summer.

When the elements of life offer us their friendship so we can continue to exist, some of us graciously agree to dance with them, but others of us refuse such friendly offers. Then, the elements of life can express their disappointment: fires burn our memories, our dreams are drowned by tsunamis, and earthquakes bury our souls.

Some of us learn from the endless lessons of life. Although we are mortals in this infinity, those lessons never stop repeating or returning. However, some people stay asleep; they are not interested in waking up. They miss the train of opportunities. They remain within the boundaries of the same station. While they continue to sleep under the lightless stars, many trains come and go. These people merely sit there and count the trains they have missed. **This illusion called life never stops digging holes for us to fall into, but it also builds mountains we can climb.** While some of us fall deeper into the darkness, others rise all the way to the top and touch the light. People receive their own version of this gift. Some of us feel content with this gift, but some feel defeated, because they don't like the paper in which life is wrapped. No grape will taste the same, and no tear will fall with the same weight. Some of us will tango with the darkness, and some of us will deliver the light.

There is happiness in the clouds, but those clouds seem to have abandoned some meadows where people only plant sorrow. In those fields, there will be no sunflowers growing: the soil is made out of tar. Those people continue to harvest whatever the day brings. Sometimes, they catch a tiny fish from their sea of hope. More often, though, they are empty-handed when they return home. Their homes are built on the broken bones of their ancestors. As if under a family curse, all they seem to inherit is a little soup of sorrow in which to dip the bruised pieces of their broken hearts. When they rise in the morning to the laughter of hyenas, they don't even look around to see if they have any wood to start the fire, since they continue to believe the flames in their hearts are nothing but snowflakes.

In these lands, people linger among the shadows of their defeats. Children play in the void; mothers' tears fall on frozen faces; and fathers fight with the ocean monsters to defend their life. However, even in that void, children never give up flying their kites. They are the real warriors of this life, because they still remember how little time they have left before they, too, fall into the oblivion of life, the way so many grown-ups have fallen. However, that magnetic emptiness starts to flirt with us. It does not discriminate by what you look like or where you come from. In this world, even if you are a blueblood, you have the same privilege as anyone else to climb up and the same opportunity to fall down.

Even the people who breathe sorrow in and out will have a chance to listen to a different song, when their time comes. They can choose to turn the volume up; they can also turn it down. We always have choices to make in this life. Someone may choose to believe that the ground they stand on is made of tar. They may believe no flowers can ever grow in such poisonous fields. But flowers are like children: they are rebellious and resilient. They can grow in every season and even through concrete. Is it possible that children do not recognize fear until they are taught to be afraid? Could it be because fear cannot occupy a seat that is filled with laughter, hope, and joy?

Children become like centuries-old trees when they lose their ground and everything starts to disappear. Under their little feet, they build the strongest roots of the human spirit. No earthquake can break them apart, no tornadoes can destroy them, no fire can come close, and no tsunamis are high enough.

When it comes to learning in this life, we need to acknowledge the children of our planet. They would never judge based on race or color, if it weren't for the adults.

Perhaps we trade in our resilience in order to grow up. We buy the secrets of being happy whenever we want through the empty promises of adulthood. We should remember the beauty of our childhood memories, especially when the winters of our adulthood bully the other seasons.

There is constant change in life. However, our boredom slows the metabolism of our perception. When we think nothing has changed, on the contrary everything changes. We change through all the paths of our lives. Regardless whether the path is familiar or not or whether we want to go with the flow or not, once we are in the stream, each one of us will change, too.

This change cannot be witnessed, however, if you are sleepwalking. You will continue to see whatever makes itself visible to you, but there are other things that cannot be seen right away. Your mind will keep track of the incidents you experience and will also create new scenarios for you to play in. For some of us, the stream can be muddy, and for some of us, it can be clear. But all of the streams, regardless of where they originate or how they travel, merge into one ocean. In that ocean, some travelers will be helped by dolphins while some will be drowned by sirens.

Many of us live our lives in isolation, far away even from ourselves. We spend a lifetime building relationships with others, but only a few of us work on our relationship with ourselves. Some people think they can get away with breaking someone's heart. Some think nothing can break their heart. Some reap what they never planted, while others only plant but never reap.

This life is like being in a stream that continuously branches out into many other rivers. With every turn, you come closer to filling the unwritten pages of your life's book. Some believe those pages were already filled; it was their destiny. They believe you only live a version of a life designed for you before your arrival. They surrender without questioning or understanding what is happening. They do not explore the possibilities of living in any other parts of the stream. Some of us wonder about the other branches of the stream, including how it all had started and where the flow is going.

In this life, there is something called "*cause and effect*." When humans are conditioned by their fear, it can push them to choose "*passing responsibility*" over "*taking responsibility*." However, it is not so easy to escape your inner judge, the voice that keeps you awake at night and makes your heart pump the blood of guilt with each restless breath you take. Is there a way to ignore the guilt?

In the streams of life, you may come across beautiful flowers; some are very fragrant but have thorns; some have overlooked healing powers and are considered weeds.

You may not always be able to reap what you sow. Your vision of justice under the law of cause and effect may never be realized. You may witness some getting a head start, while you feel held back by the chains of your destiny.

There are some who believe that you create your destiny. There are those who leave their fate in the hands of their Creator. In a world where opposites never exit the dance floor and everyone is used to wearing masks, nobody can really be sure who their dance partner is. You could be doing your tango with either the darkness or the light. At the critical moment of choosing your partner, you begin the process of the cause and effect.

The energy of any choice you make can transform itself into anything. When you step away from being true, you open many doors into the garden of illusions. In this garden, you eat the poisonous apple from the tree of disillusionment. While you enjoy eating the poisoned apple, you may think you are awake when, in fact, you are sleeping. In your state of sleepwalking, you can indeed continue your life and even achieve more of your dreams, while still dreaming. That way, you may even believe you are conscious. However, what you need to know is that when your consciousness is held hostage by the subconscious mind, your life is nothing but a dream within a dream.

But the mind is such an ornery player. You can never be entirely sure that the record being played over and over again in your mind is yours. Perhaps your perception of life is also an illusion within the impermanence of life: nothing remains the same, and everything experiences continuous transformation.

In the cycles of change, some of us trade places unexpectedly, and our lives become a movie we watch. It can be difficult to witness your own life falling into pieces, when it seems your curse will never break. We grow older in our garden of youth. We think it is too late to go after our dreams. So, we choose to sit on the bench, procrastinating.

However, the birds of dreamers are not meant to live in cages. They need to fly freely. That is their agreement with life. Fish will swim, grass will grow, flowers will bloom, and they all will continue to transform. But where do our tears go? How about our unfilled dreams and indelible disappointments? Is there a universal pawnshop?

Is there a place where people can get their second chances in life? Or is it a human agreement about life that he strikes just once and he is out? Where does someone go when he is lost? Is there any water in the universe where lost souls can wash away their sorrows and then rediscover their hopes? Perhaps not everyone walks into the stream voluntarily. Some of us question whether we really asked for the life we have and, if we did, where we went wrong. And when someone is drowning in their suffering, they usually are not thinking about the color of the ocean they are about to dive into.

Somehow, life on this planet has been initiated. If someone or something has arranged this experience called *life*, surely they did not send us here with instructions, as we seem to have been left to our own devices. So, when we need an answer, we want to hear it from above, because we think there has to be a beginning for all of this.

Whether we chose to be here voluntarily or not, life is happening with us in it or without us. There is a brilliant plan beyond our comprehension that keeps the engine of life going. It may seem to end for one individual, but life itself continues. The energy is transformed. But why should we wait until we are dead for our energy to change?

If something can shift and if we believe we can make that shift, why should we not just do it?

Fear holds us back. The mind deals us many hands. In the game you play, you are not the only participant. What does it take for someone to wake up? If there is a plan, then perhaps there is a possibility of our falling asleep. There should also be plan B, in case of experiencing sleepwalking. Should it not be? Would this great project simply go to waste? Would it not defeat its purpose?

Perhaps the screenplay of life indeed was co-written by opposites. We read the lines assigned to us and find our role comes easily to us at that precise moment. But what about making an unexpected mistake because that is what the script says? That would take the fun out of life. Otherwise, we would never be imaginative. Does it not start with the imagination? How do we keep on going?

Perhaps we, too, are included in that screenplay. Maybe we say, "If I am going to play, then I get to choose, too."

Indeed.

When we think of the darkness, we get blinded by the perception created by our upbringing. We think when darkness falls and rains on us, no more light can shine through the gray clouds. We forget that even the hidden shade of darkness has a spot where light is always invited in. There is always room for light in the darkness.

We often question why we are here. We often feel we need to know why. There has to be a reason for all of this, especially the suffering we experience. For so many of us, suffering never ends; it just changes its costume to appear different to us. But it's not hard for us to recognize the sadness, when our hearts ache uncontrollably. When we are sad, the child's laughter remains hidden behind the walls of our broken faith. Our hands are paralyzed, and we fail to unlock the iron gates of suffering.

So why are we here? To experience suffering and then, perhaps, happiness?

Life is a verb. It gets designed and redesigned constantly. It is a bridge between reality and delusion. It is an ocean where anything can swim in harmony and where anything can also get caught outside of it. In this water, life is created and finds its way. Some rivers reach the deepest part of the forest, and some rivers come down from the highest peaks of the mountains. Life finds its way from any direction. Each path creates a new journey.

One of our meditation teachers once told us that we do not notice things around us when we are falling out of a tree. All we can comprehend at first is that we have fallen. We do not notice the leaves on the tree or the animals in its branches during our fall, because the fall *does not occur in slow motion*. We do not have the luxury of slowing down our fall to see what else is happening around us.

I loved his analogy. When we are falling or walking on a path that will create suffering for us, we do not get the opportunity to rewind the record of our actions so we can watch it in slow motion. Only then, perhaps, might we be able to realize what we've done that we could have done differently. But when we do not have an awareness of what's happening to us at the moment, we continue to fall down many trees at the speed of light, and we keep landing on the same hard surfaces. This is how we get caught in cycles of stupidity. We continue to sleepwalk, and we fall down multiple trees.

It would be so beneficial for us, if we came with some kind of recognition device built inside us. Perhaps, when we were about to make a mistake that would cause suffering for us or others, it would zap us so rapidly, we would never even think about being that foolish again.

Oh! *Wait!* Maybe we *do* have that device installed in us already. How about common sense? How about becoming aware of what is right and what is wrong? How about being here right now instead of being stuck in the past or getting lost in the future? How about that?

What happens to those of us who fall? Are we caught in the sticky, lacy eyelashes of spiders? Are our minds penetrated by toxic shine of poison ivy leaves? Are our hopes stolen by crows and fed to their babies? Does the rain fall so heavily on us that our hearts are crushed? Do we grow so far apart from ourselves that we forget about our childhood? What happens to us when we hit the ground?

Could this possibly have been written in the skies? Could this possibly have been chosen for us, as if our lives were predestined? As human beings, there has to be a time and a place where we claim responsibility for our actions. **We need to learn to release ourselves from suffering.** But suffering is just like falling down a tree: you don't notice when the pain is activated; and you don't see the severity of it until you hit the ground and your heart breaks into thousands of pieces. That is when you need to know that the stars above represent all the lights within all the hopeless pieces of every broken heart.

This is to show us that, if gravity can make you fall, then your hopes can lift you up to rise above anything. However, this will not be apparent to you if you are sleepwalking.

Then how do we wake up and realize we are actually awake? How do we accept the life we have as it is and live at peace? How do we stop the urge to change everything and everyone around us because they don't satisfy us? How do we start living only in this moment?

Your life is happening right now.

Are we born into this life completely stripped of our memories? Is life a mischievous dance partner who changes steps and moves unexpectedly?

Life is a dance that takes place between the light and the dark. Sometimes you dance in complete darkness. Even then, you continue dancing because you can still hear the music in your heart. The challenge begins when you can no longer hear the music. Life's music is like food for us. Some of us take it for granted and feed our demons with it. Some of us feed others and then ourselves. Some of us add our own ingredients to spice it up. Some of us do not want to consume it all, so we save it for later. Maybe I will do this after I graduate or after I retire. Maybe I will go there after the kids grow up or get married. Maybe… Maybe... Maybe… Then the food expires.

What is keeping us alive then? What is our will to survive? Why do some of us believe they have had enough of it and decide to end it in the middle of their spring? Why do some of us feel entitled to steal it from others? Why do some of us remain paralyzed in fear, sitting on our couches and watching television for hours while we criticize what we watch? Why are we throwing this gift away by sleepwalking? Why are we not waking up?

How would you know if you were awakened? Would the colors around you change?

2

RISE AND SHINE, MY ABSENT MIND

AWAKENING STARTS with being true to yourself. Every time you play the role that comes with the identity you have created or borrowed or stolen, you unconsciously take another sleeping pill. The longer you continue to remain hidden and lost in your own illusion, the faster you buy in to everyone else's delusion. You buy season tickets to the shows presented by illusionists performing with the ghosts of lost souls. And you do not realize that, in your paralyzed mind and body, your soul has indeed been lost, too.

Even then, you will have options. You can continue to watch the same channel, listen to the same song, read the same paragraph, and have the same conversation again. Or you can choose to wake up. Those who recognize they are suffering but do nothing about it are unconscious. When you shift the gear into neutral, you will notice that things slow down. Remember the story about falling down a tree? How much do you think you would notice if your fall occurred in really slow motion? If you do not stand still, you will miss out more. If you do all the talking, you will not hear what others say.

Awakening is not about recognizing or adopting any identity. In fact, awakening is not about your identity at all. Being true to yourself is something that can only be defined and exercised by you. Being real means you do not become just anyone in order to please others or fit in. Do you know if you are true to yourself or not?

Do you remember the recognition device I mentioned earlier? In this case, that device does exist. It actually zaps you when you are not true to yourself. Because human beings can be such brick walls sometimes, unfortunately we may miss the first zapping. These are the times when people keep complaining about how they keep making the same mistakes, as if those nauseating patterns were created by others, not by themselves.

When we miss the first zapping, our physical body will dial you "via collect call." Do not even consider failing to pick up that phone or refusing that collect call. Because, if you don't, that will be your second strike. Who knows: your ignorance can even invite the third strike. *That* strike is an eye opener: your doctor may give you the bad news, your relationship can come to an end, you may lose what you have, and/or your life can become unfamiliar to you.

Relax. This does not have to be bad at all, so long as you know what to do.

This is for those who are not true to themselves, who are not paying attention and being ignorant. They continue to fall down the tree until they fall on their faces on concrete, their reality hardened by the humility they much need.

Do we really need harsh lessons and suffering to wake up? Seriously?

Yes, apparently we do. Because we will not proactively find ways to end suffering before it begins unless we get kicked out of our comfort zones, until the ones we take for granted leave us, and until we lose what we have. After all, we were taught to let sleeping dogs lie.

However, your suffering does not automatically qualify you for a free ticket to the land of the awakened ones. So you need to be aware of those who suffer. If you are the one who is suffering, do not label yourself as a victim. Anyone who has the opportunity to learn during their lifetime will have to face some degree of suffering. If everything falls into your lap easily, you may not understand the value of it. But you should not go out and create suffering for yourself or others, either.

When you recognize suffering, your energy will change. Unfortunately, others can also notice. When someone suffers, they can invite heaviness wherever they go. Not everyone is equipped with wisdom and experience to handle such energy. Many find it suffocating, so it is easier for them to walk away or remain silent. They may not know how to help you. You may feel abandoned.

Unfortunately, some people will be interested in hearing about the mistakes you make. They may want to know how and why you've done something, instead of offer their help to you.

Perhaps it is better this way. Let go of anyone who chooses not be there for you. We all get opportunities. Some of us use them wisely. Some of us are afraid to use them.

Just remember: suffering is for everyone. Do not compare yours to others. So what are you going to do with that suffering of yours?

Imagine what being awake means. What is the difference between those who are aware of their suffering and those who are not? Notice the ones who act like victims and those who are committed to learning from their suffering.

Suffering cannot be ignored. You cannot avoid it. It will exercise its journey on the pathway designed only by you. This is the biggest difference between those who are aware of their experience versus those who are not. You actually have the power to find ways to end your suffering. First of all, just recognize it as the way it is. Do not label it. Do not color it. Do not ignore it. Just acknowledge the fact that you are suffering. Do not try to find a reason for it. Do not try to bury it. Do not try to freeze it. Do not try to burn it. Simply accept that you are suffering.

You will know it because your heart will ache. You will know it because you will feel like everyone else is moving on but you. You will know it because you will feel like you have lost your wings, your hopes and dreams. You will know it because the darkness will start to flirt with you. Even then, you have to remember that nothing is permanent. Yes, you can find ways to end your suffering.

Remember the first step?

Recognize and accept your suffering for what it is. Do not ask the question why, because it will reveal itself to you, when you are committed to being a good student. While this happens, your senses will continue to trick you. The most challenging of all is the mind. Your mind can take you to the darkest corners of life, when you are not aware.

Your tongue is another important thing to watch. Simply put, the more you talk about it, especially in the form of blame (as if your suffering was caused by others), the deeper the hole you will dig, burying your chances of waking up. So, keep your mouth tamed when the urge arises to blame someone or something else. Do you know why? Because it does not matter. Blaming others will only reinforce your victim-energy state of being, and it will not make your suffering go away. If you feel like talking, then start practicing loving kindness. **Be the messenger of right speech**. Speak only kind words.

Your eyes will also play tricks on you. You may only see other people being happy, yet you feel sad. You will see others moving on, yet you are stuck. You will see only what the victim is willing to see. How about seeing children at play? How about noticing a stranger helping other strangers? How about a neighbor giving a flower to her neighbor? Remember, you can choose what you want to see. Then, **have the right view**.

Your ears will test you, too. You will start to practice selective hearing. You will hear more of what is not fair versus what is pleasing. Your ears will accept any invitation coming from the Department of Gossip. When this happens, **choose to hear the truth**.

Your sense of smell will pass by the roses but capture the rotten unfairness of your life. You will forget you still can choose the smell of beautiful flowers any time you want. You will connect to those smells associated with memories where you remain stuck. Go ahead and **smell the roses** instead.

And touch. This one can break down walls, if you choose to receive the support of others. Humans are energetic beings. Touch can activate the right connection between all of your senses. Touch is also about you. Do not lose your connection. **Keep in touch with** yourself.

Now that you have accepted the fact that you are suffering, **do not be too quick to judge anyone or anything, including yourself.** Do not try to solve or find a reason for your pain right away. Do not compare your suffering to everyone else's. Try to remember that everyone has their own version of suffering.

So what should you do? First, ask yourself this: Are you in this situation because of *you*? If you say "no," you are either still not aware, or you are simply not telling the truth. Because, no matter how unfair it may seem to you, *you* are the main reason for your suffering, and you are also the main power to lessen it or even end it.

Unless you truly believe there might be a silver lining to the mistakes you've made, your suffering will linger. Your suffering may have nothing at all to do with you, personally. You may be a compassionate person who suffers because there is so much hunger on our planet. But how is your suffering going to find a solution that can end the hunger problem?

So, **find a way to channel the energy you put into suffering instead into the cessation of suffering.** If you were the one who made a mistake, acted stupidly, or did the wrong thing, then simply confess. Do not lie about it any longer. Not telling the truth will consume so much of your energy. Reveal the truth and set yourself free. If you suffer because of others, then how do you set yourself free?

This is when "compassion" takes the driver's seat. Compassion is one of the gifts we human beings have. Let it create a warm blanket and a helping hand for those who need it. **Be compassionate.** Because, when you are, your actions will change the frequency, which will bring balance back into your life. Compassion feeds harmony in life. If there is no harmony, you will either hear only the frogs or only the crickets on long summer nights. In truth, those creatures make up the most harmonious couple of summer. They always take turns. Just listen to them.

Your compassion for life will help lighten up someone else's suffering. When you suffer, you can become more compassionate and kind toward others and to yourself. It will become easier to recognize others' pain. You have an ideal opportunity to utilize your senses. Let your senses help you to channel your goodness everywhere. Become the healer you were meant to be. Use your kindness to lift up someone's spirit.

So, suffering does not have to be bad at all. Just remember that nothing is permanent and everything changes. You are the main force for making these shifts. You are the deciding factor for how long your suffering lasts. It is up to you how long you want to suffer.

If you get sucked into the never-ending, bewitching elixir of pain because it keeps you in a coma, you may never wake up in this lifetime. This is a form of sleepwalking. Instead of learning from your experience, you will steer away from being true to yourself. You will think you are fooling everyone else, but indeed you know who the biggest fool really is. **Be true to yourself and others**.

When you help others, regardless how little or extensively, it will help you in return. When you get out of your drama to volunteer for a cause, this helps you, too.

This journey, however, is not easy. It will test you constantly. There may even be moments where you lose your faith in yourself and in life. That moment, however, is the turning point of your life. The decision to choose between the light and the dark could be a great opportunity for you. When we suffer, it feels dark. When we are in pain, it feels dark. When we are sad and lonely, it feels dark. If the darkness is all that your senses can detect, how are you going to find the light in that dark universe of yours?

To begin with, you share this life. The universe you live in also belongs to others. Then, logically, can everyone be in the same darkness at the same time? Is this possible? Just like our planet continues to spin and faces both the sun and the moon, you, too, are always turning. Both light and dark surround you.

It is like playing a game with two teams. Some of us are in the dark, and some of us are in the light. Choose your team. Also, try this: see if you can be hopeless and hopeful at the very same time. I mean in the exact identical millisecond. Your thoughts and emotions can shift from one second to next. But you can never have two exact opposite feelings or thoughts within your body, mind, and soul at the exact same time. So you have to choose.

Maybe it is all about the choices, then. Isn't it?

Let's make this more interesting. Both sides have recruiters, headhunters, messengers, angels, delivery drivers, sign carriers, and so on. Both sides can shift their shape to become anything or anyone at any time. The dark side is good at acting like the light, in order to get closer to you. Welcome to having a human experience!

Then how can we recognize them?

Let's remember the recognition device, and this time this device goes beyond your insight and intuition. It is called *wisdom*. In life, knowledge will guide and help you to have a successful journey. Without wisdom, your chances are as good as a leaf blowing around in a hurricane. You would not know where you were. You would not understand the cause of your suffering. You would miss the signs and get recruited by the dark side.

3

HUMAN RESOURCES OF THE DARK SIDE

ONCE YOUR RÉSUMÉ of stupidity and ignorance gets delivered to the Human Resources Department in the dark side, here is what the cover letter reads:

> *I have no wisdom, but I act as I have it. I do all the talking, and I never listen. I never learn from the mistakes I have made, because I know it all. If I feel stressed, I can always go back to sleep by eating or intoxicating myself excessively. Just like I said, "I know it all." Please hire me.*

Good news! You are hired. Just like that. Instantly!

The dark side not only will hire you, but it will also support you by providing a lifetime of sleeping pills.

But how do you know you are now living in the dark side?

First, your body will tell you. But there is also a probation period. You might not know about this, because it was agreed upon by the directors of the union created by the dark and the light side. According to an agreement they signed, everybody deserves a chance, an opportunity to wake up.

The probation period is not the same for everyone, however. It will entirely be up to you how you perform during this time. However, there is always an end to it. The dark side will never terminate your employment. The light side will never stop trying to get you back. Because your core self, upon its arrival on this planet for its human experience, was also sponsored by the light. If you do not wake up, the dark will continue rocking you to sleep. It will feed you with the milk of illusions. You will be wrapped in the blanket of delusions during cold winters. You will be served cold lemonade made of the fruits of confusion in hot summer days. Of course, you will not notice any of this.

The good news is that wisdom is not selective or prejudiced. So we all have the opportunity to earn it. Here is the challenge: While the light will encourage you to earn wisdom, the dark will distract you. The light will put up road signs for you, but the dark will spray paint over them. The light will encourage you to take the stairs to help your heart, but the dark will pick you up at your door in a stretch limo or on a flying carpet.

The road on the light side will never remain unlit. Because that is how you can always find your way back: the light will not abandon you. But it is you who need to find it and commit to it. Then, the wisdom will start to run in your blood. The light will find its home in your eyes. Living beings will be attracted to you. Your wisdom will no longer be for you alone. You will channel it to guide others. You will know by then that your suffering indeed was for a reason. It is your place to shine.

In this life, you will be exposed to every season's everchanging colors and stories. But you will not be able to remember everything you have experienced. You simply will not have enough time to remember. Perhaps you should pay closer attention to people who walk into your life. How about the things you have lived and witnessed? Do you think it is time for you to sit down and think about your life? Do you know where you are and where you are going? Does your existence in this place matter?

Yes, it does matter. You matter. You do not have to have an out-of-body experience to see yourself. You are more than you think you are. But this is not about identity. Just remember and repeat, repeat, and repeat, "**Identity is an experience**." You do not have to purchase or create any character. Just remember that.

Also, remember that the Human Resources of the Dark Side will keep your résumé on their file until your time is up on this planet.

Some even believe that your résumé follows you to your next life, as well. I believe you had better finish anything unfinished while you are in this life, so you do not have to worry about it anymore. Do not become the ghost of an incomplete life. Do not get stuck between lives. Do not waste your life.

Because once the darkness finds out that you are still insisting on keeping your identity, not only will it create the perfect job for you, but it will also give you the corner office.

The honeymoon period of your employment with the dark side will be fantastic. You will be drugged and intoxicated. Not only will everything look so cool; you will also get really high without wings. You will continue to sleepwalk, but, after your honeymoon ends, your dreams will become your reality. Your reality will give birth to your suffering. And your suffering can either wake you up or put you back to sleep.

Most of us, before accepting an employment offer from the dark side, get a feeling in our physical body. It's usually in the solar plexus area, where the network of nerves behind the stomach begins to screech. However, due to our ignorant pride, we seem to hear nothing, which confuses our cells, as if we have deceived them. It is like your guard dog starts to bark, letting you know there is an intruder in the house, but you not only tell your dog to be quiet but also put a muzzle on him. Why would you sabotage yourself? What is the offer from the darkness that you cannot resist? How is it logical to believe in that, when the darkness is selling time-shares in the island of enlightenment?

It is a bit dysfunctional to ignore our intuition. Sometimes we set ourselves up to inhale the fumes of darkness in order to learn from our ignorance. When we learn to see the light, we can help others become aware of it, too.

Gaining employment in the darkness is actually like losing part of your common sense. Perhaps, the law of cause and effect is fathomable to those whose logic has been fed only empty promises. When does someone actually look at their paycheck from an employer, "The Darkness, Inc.," and realize they have not made any money? How can someone actually wake up and understand that the Human Resources Department for Darkness, Inc. does not provide any services for your wellbeing? Can you terminate your employment with the darkness?

Yes, you can.

Once you start to see the results of your employment by the darkness, reactions will occur in your physical body. You remember your solar plexus, right? It is payback time. You remember your guard dog, right? Get ready to be bitten. After your initial reaction, which will most likely consist of lots of anger, you will unwillingly learn to calm down. That will start your journey toward your healing.

So, it does not have to be the end of your life, if you have made a mistake and ended up working for the darkness. Those who take the job still have the potential to be hired by the light. Be wise. Do not miss this opportunity.

4

TANGO OF WISDOM AND COMPASSION

THERE WILL COME a time in your life when you will no longer need to know why certain things happened to you the way they did. You will see this when you take *"I," "me," "my,"* and *"mine"* out of the equation. You will end up with the concept of *"selflessness."* Congratulations! You have just arrived at the doorstep of *"wisdom hood."* Come over and knock on its door.

Gaining wisdom starts with selflessness. Can you handle it? This means you do not get attached to the identity you think you have. You also need to tame your sense of self somewhat. Eventually, you will have to learn to let go of the self. However, this does not mean you will be lost in the diabolical seas of the human experience. If you are never lost, you'll never know what other versions of you might be found. How about becoming the best version of you?

This is an opportunity to revise yourself. This is how you get dissected. This is how the illusion of having an identity loses its empty power. This is how you are stripped of the mask you wear to hide your face. This is how the world gets to meet your pure version of you.

Wisdom is not prejudicial against anyone. It is available for everyone. It cannot be purchased. It cannot be rented. Your pride may steer you away from it, but humility may lead you right back to it. Satisfying your ego may cause you to take the long path to it, but selflessness may carry you directly to it. Ignorance may not bring you to it, but compassion may guide you to it. Delusion may keep you away from it, but being in the moment may keep you connected to it.

Someone else's wisdom can only help you if you are willing to learn from it. Everyone's journey is personal.

On our journey to our self-discovery, sometimes we have to walk on thin bridges, and some of us will fall off as we try to reach our destination. It would be a great benefit for you to learn from the experience of falling.

When you realize there is no other way to go but up, you will resist the urge to go to sleep by being ignorant. It is like being in the freezing cold: you can no longer take it. Your eyes want to shut, and your blood does not want to run. You just want to sleep, as your body turns blue and you feel numb. If you could only close your eyes and go to sleep for a short while, then everything would be just fine when you wake up…

But you never wake up from that sleep. Ignorance cannot stop the snowflakes from falling on your frozen body.

Do you think the light will not try to wake you up?

When you think sleeping is a good idea when you are about to freeze, are you receiving advice from the dark? When you see a bird feather falling among the snowflakes, are you receiving a message from the light? How would you know which side is sending you messages?

Every time you experience the darkness, you actually get closer to becoming wiser. This is, of course, not going to work for everyone. Some of us still touch the hot stove again and again. And as long as they live, there will be many more "hot stove" incidents which are never our fault, because we are so attached to our victim identity. The victim state of mind never takes responsibility. It is always someone *else's* fault, because it was this and it was that. Victims will remain victims as long as they ignore the fact that they are sleepwalking.

Let's create a theorem by combining wisdom, compassion, and intellect:

Compassion - Wisdom = Absentminded person who has a heart of gold

Wisdom - Compassion = Mindful person who has a heart of stone

Wisdom + Compassion =Your ticket to awakening

So, if you are sleepwalking, you most likely lack *both* wisdom and compassion. People who are only watering the intellectual side of their garden will likely harvest the rotten fruit of pride and ego. Individuals who are only watering the compassion side of their garden will likely reap lots of fruit and give them to everyone else. There is nothing wrong with such noble act of compassion, as long as you are not avoiding your own being. Intellectuals will try to be fair, so they will count the world population and divide their fruit evenly, including to themselves. Compassionate ones will hand-deliver that fruit, even on an empty stomach.

In life, we need the characteristics of *both*, if we are looking for bliss. We need to be **mindful**, but that alone will not help us gain wisdom. We *also* need to be **compassionate**. And, usually, compassion comes with love, kindness, humility, and suffering.

Wisdom may also come with suffering. Then, would it be incorrect to say that suffering can actually take you to bliss?

Suffering can open for you the doors to the gardens of both the intellectuals and the compassionate ones. There, you will be exposed to the cycles of thought and emotion, birth and death. During suffering, you will go through a lot of emotion. Many thoughts will visit you without your even knowing. So it is very likely you could feel that your entire existence has been invaded. You are no longer in control. Your mind will go in every direction, acknowledging each and every feeling. Until the storms of your own confusion settle, your ship of peace will not sail on these upside down waters. If there is no calm in your mind, wisdom cannot find its way. If there is no room left in your heart, compassion cannot find its way.

So, suffering should be seen as an opportunity, not as the curse of some unlucky soul. It is not about luck or curses. It is not about desiring or avoiding. It is about acknowledging what it is. It is about making a commitment to your present moment. It is about being mindful and compassionate. It is about recognizing the beauty in this life, despite its ugliness. It is about making the right choices.

Wisdom and compassion never travel far away from each other. However, neither one can be injected into anyone for a quick fix. Suffering can help you to earn both, so long as you are willing to learn from it. If you want to start, then you have to let go of the identity you have adopted.

5

TOUCHING THE NEEDLE OF THE SPINNING WHEEL

MOST OF US know the fairytale about the princess who pricked her finger on a spindle and fell asleep. Apparently, the spell she fell under was stronger than all the preventative measures devised to protect her.

Although it is a fairytale, some parts should raise questions. Is it possible that some things in life are predetermined, and, no matter what you do, you can never escape from them or stop them from happening? What are your thoughts about this?

Does it mean there might be other forces that have control over your life?

The biggest difference between someone who acts like a victim and someone who does not is the **taking of ownership**. Regardless of whether you find yourself in a situation that has occurred by no direct fault of your own, you still have the freedom to perceive whatever is happening. Thinking about the past or the future instead of being in the moment will not help you move forward. You need to see your situation from a different angle. This is a good step to take toward wisdom. If the way you have been thinking has not helped you, in a particular situation, then you have to change your thought process.

Here is a good lesson: Do not assume anything. You need to move closer to the truth, not further away from it. But if you do not know what is happening, can you still know what to do next? And if you make assumptions, do you think you have all the facts?

When you sincerely do not know what is happening, don't do anything except breathe until you are calm. Your first responsibility is to breathe! Do not try to figure out why whatever happened to you has happened. Regardless of whether it was your fault or not, still just focus on your breathing. Your breath will be your anchor.

When your fear creates tornados, your breath will ground you. Breathe...

When your anxiety cuts off your wings, your breath will help you rise above. Breathe...

When your depression invites vultures to stand over your body, your breath will turn them into butterflies. Breathe...

You need to breathe to stay alive. If you can't breathe, you really do not need to worry about being wise or not.

Your wisdom can help more people when you are alive. Breathe...

Being calm will change your frequency. Not feeling calm is similar to walking on a thin bridge built between the highest mountains. So relax and stay calm. You will feel safe once you realize the ground under you is no longer falling apart. Sometimes, we are the ones who create earthquakes and rock our own worlds.

Wisdom can be developed based on how you choose to live, where and with whom you hang out, what you do for a living, your thought processes, your perception, your responses versus your reactions, and much more. And wisdom does not have to be so difficult to acquire.

Here are some of the things that may help you to achieve some wisdom:

- ❖ Again, **never assume anything.** Assumptions are poisonous and will dump you halfway. You will fall on your face in the middle of the road. When you assume, your mind starts to play the other person's part. You think you know the other person's part and what they are thinking. Instead, *ask* the other person. Do not assume.
- ❖ **Do not act like you know it all.** Because you don't. Nobody does.
- ❖ **Do not judge.** Who do you think you are? Everyone has a story. You cannot possibly know everything about another person's story.
- ❖ **Do not be the victim of your drama.** In fact, do not feed into any drama. You can become what you feed. And what you feed can learn to consume you like food, too.
- ❖ When you take care of yourself, remember you are an energetic being with intellectual, physical, emotional, and spiritual component parts. So **make sure you are balanced.**
- ❖ **Do not try to prove your point of view.** Remember that your point of view is as pointless as the other person's point of view, when you two are in an argument. In war, nobody wins.
- ❖ **Listen more and talk less.**
- ❖ **Spend less time in front of the television.**
- ❖ **Enjoy more time in nature.**
- ❖ **Devote more time to children and elders.**
- ❖ **Donate.**
- ❖ **Volunteer.**
- ❖ **Dance, sing, paint, write, read, and walk.**
- ❖ **Practice meditation.**
- ❖ **Help others.**

While you try to earn some wisdom, the darkness is not just going to take a back seat. While you suffer, you may experience abandonment. Some of your friends may seem distant to you. Let them stay there. It is up to you. It is your life.

The darkness will do anything to consume you. It will support your sadness by removing you from your friends. It will make you feel drained so you don't want to do anything but sleep. It will also push you into a corner so deeply, you may even consider ending your own life.

Breathe....

Remember how both sides have recruiters? Living a happy, peaceful, joyful, and healthy life is not just for *some* people. It is okay to send good thoughts to *everyone,* so all beings may be happy.

- ❖ Choose goodness over viciousness.
- ❖ Choose forgiveness over revenge.
- ❖ Choose love over fear.
- ❖ Let go of anger.
- ❖ Let go of stubbornness.
- ❖ Let go of despair.

Suffering can heal your life if you are acutely aware of it and willing to learn from it.

Then why are we so stubborn and proudly stupid? What is the reward for such resistance to our own healing, if there even is one?

When you look around, you will see many beings from many different backgrounds and places. What I am about to say is just a theory.

I think, when we come here to have this experience called life, we are equipped with a certain amount of storage or memory space, just like computers.

Imagine for a minute that we are not alone in this universe. Imagine a classroom-like setting where the elderly talk about a very special place called "Earth." The elders describe the internship opportunities on planet Earth. Once the excitement spreads among the novices, they all raise their hands to volunteer to be sent to planet Earth. However, the darkness is also aware of this opportunity. Could you find any more perfect place than our world for the light and the dark to dance together?

Just like computers, there is a storage capacity limit. Before we take off to visit the planet Earth, we are all given a to-do list.

Anything else you do may be extra-credit or cause you to lose an earned credit.

We all receive the same speech. It includes the words "cause and effect," "free will," and "common sense," but you will not be able to remember it all. Once you leave home and arrive at the planet, the only thing stuck in your head is this:

> *Collect data while you are there. Do not forget when someone tells you something you've never heard before. Record it. Make sure the data is not breached. Collect data.*
>
> *Oh! One more thing. You are not the data you collected.*

Guess which one of the messages we forget as soon as we arrive here?

This is how we start forming an identity. You hear for the first time when some family member says, *"You are fat," "You are ugly,"* or *"You are worthless!"*

What do you think your child version will do in response to this? *"I am fat," "I am ugly,"* and *"I am worthless."* Check that the information has been received and recorded in the data bank. I have to make sure I never stop believing it. These are now my beliefs, and they are true. They cannot be changed.

Great! You have just swallowed three sleeping pills...

So you get the picture. Every time you record a dysfunctional belief and believe it to be true, you take a sleeping pill.

When you grow older, you become more proud and protective of your beliefs, certain they are true.

And who do you think sponsors your dysfunctional beliefs during your lifetime? The darkness? Or the light?

So, actually, the more sleeping pills you swallow, the further from gaining wisdom you will be. Most of us, however, take those pills unconsciously. We don't know we are taking them, because our ego, pride, values, sense of self, our assumed identity, and so many other beliefs prevent us from seeing things clearly.

When clarity is in the hands of the darkness, you will lose all colors except gray. You will fall into a place called *"the waiting room of the sleepwalkers"* and will not even know why you are there or for whom you are waiting.

6

THE WAITING ROOM OF THE
SLEEPWALKERS

THIS ROOM HAS multiple televisions with programs and infomercials designed to put you into a hypnotic state of mind. They also offer a continuous stream of consumer offers with no interest fees or down payments for anything you purchase. You know what is happening here, right?

Sleepwalkers are in a rat race with their friends, neighbors, colleagues, and even their families. They want to earn the Consumer of the Year Award. They are more interested in hearing about what kind of shoes celebrities purchase than in taking a deep breath. They are willing to do anything to get a promotion so they can make more money and buy the knock-off version of shoes a celebrity has purchased.

They will not listen to you when you call them out. They may volunteer for a good cause, but only because it will look good on their résumés. They will be devastated when they cannot get the newest version of a high-tech product before it is offered to the general public.

The sleepwalkers believe they are better than others. In the street, they capture trendy cars using their high-tech devices, but they miss their children's first words or steps. They will argue with you until the cows come home, however, as far as they are concerned, cows will never come back. When they lose, they never comprehend why. When their dear friends leave, they think it is because of jealousy. They believe that their religion, their government, their country are the best. They continue to operate under the belief that, if it weren't for them, this world would be much worse.

By the way, that waiting room is the planet they live in. *Are you a sleepwalker?*

While you sleepwalk, anything can show up in front of you. Anything can fall onto your head, you can stumble and fall, and many more incidents can occur. Also, your loved one may wake you up in the middle of your trance.

Some of us make those things show up in front of us. We make ourselves stumble and fall. We also send messages to our loved ones to wake us up.

Some of us actually carry a high sense of duty, as if we know the reason for being here. Especially those who come here to help others: their services as light-workers and healers will be tested harder. Their duty requires a serious commitment.

Those who never seem to fall asleep will be awoken with so much noise, the ground may shake. Their suffering will be great enough to burn every tree they've watered. They will experience loneliness that makes them question the existence of light. They will feel so deceived, they may even consider ending their own human experience once and for all.

What these individuals may not know is that they have always been watched over, ever since they departed their homes and came to planet Earth.

Remember those novices? Some of them are so promising that both the darkness and the light watch them. Their mission is so big that, if they ever fall asleep, they will be reminded of their duty. They should never give up. Right before they departed, the dark gave them an intense pride, steely ego, determination, focus, intellect, and strength, so they will have an unbreakable identity. The light, on the other hand, gave them a priceless opportunity to make the stupidest mistake of their lives while sleepwalking happily as a human on planet Earth.

These select individuals have the ability to tip the balance. If they feel they were deceived and do not deserve what they are going through, anger will be their guide. If they realize this is not just about them and they learn to be true, they will be guided by the light. And their light will illuminate even those who are consumed by anger.

So ask yourself next time: Is your suffering offering you an opportunity to learn from it? Or is it some punishment, encouraging you to give up?

Suffering is experienced by all living beings based on their capacity. Where one healthy tree can be burned down by a small flame, another tree can survive a forest fire. Can they reverse the result? Can they reverse the fire?

Remember to breathe. Do not blame anyone or anything. Accept suffering as it is. Do not hurry to find a solution.

Hurrying is like trying to drink every single drop of water in an ocean. You cannot digest it. Trying to understand at the speed of light why you suffer is not going to happen. So do not hurry.

When suffering starts, you will first visit the darkness. Therefore, you will need a light so you are able to read the directions written on the labyrinths of your suffering. Just like the frogs and the crickets, the sun and the moon also live in harmony. So you have to believe that the sun will shine. You will take it one step at a time. During your journey, you can become the light you expect to find.

Become the light.

When you are in the waiting room of the sleepwalkers, can you even remember how you got there in the first place? The room's walls are made of the membranes of your carelessness. The curtains are hung by the hooks of your desires.

The best part about this waiting room is that it can become anything you are comfortable with. Your room will decorate itself based on your taste for ignorance and heedlessness. You will sit on claws in the void thinking it is the most comfortable couch. You will sip wrath in your emptiness and think you have found the Fountain of Youth. You will feed vultures with your own flesh thinking you are giving olive branches to doves. You will look at yourself in the mirror but will never see the sleeping version of yourself.

There will be others in this room who will talk about their lives. They will talk about their promotions, cars, credit scores, and also everyone else's lives, so long as they have something to gossip about. They will also mention one or two things about their political views, as well as what they do for a living. You will probably feel like you belong to that prestigious club. In fact, everyone who is sleepwalking in the heedlessness of their hollow lives is a member of this club.

The waiting room of this club can be accessed anytime by the director of the darkness. When that visit occurs, you will all receive your drink of choice. You will also be given another dose of magical sleeping pill, including higher promotions, bigger cars, better credit scores, and, of course, a full serving of gossip.

However, sometimes, some of us wake up from their sleep and leave the waiting room. What could allow us to hear the alarm clock? What is it that wakes us up?

Perhaps that internal device has been programmed to wake us up when the time is right. Is it possible that this was arranged for us? What about our free will? Do we even have free will? Is our life just a big, empty set-up?

The light will wake you up. The sun will seep through the curtains of your caprice, and your loved ones will break through the front door. The music of humility and whispers of hope will wake you up.

We end up in these waiting rooms for a reason. Unfortunately, not everyone takes the opportunity to comprehend the reason they are there, so they will visit more waiting rooms. Those who wake up will likely not visit that place again. However, some still will.

Some people will learn from their mistakes, but most will not. They will continue on their journey, sitting on a Ferris wheel, thinking they are in the room to receive the recipe for a good life.

Even though they are merely moving in circles, stuck within the boundaries of a Ferris wheel, they will *think* they are traveling between the stars.

7

WHAT DO YOU DO FOR A LIVING?

WHEN YOU ASK this question—"What do you do for a living?"—
what type of answers do you get?

> *Well, I work for so and so.*

> *I am a rocket scientist.*

> *I am a runway model.*

> *I am a professional this and that.*

Does anyone ever answer, *"Well, to begin with, I make sure that I
breathe and take care of my physical body"*? Has anyone answered you
like that?

We are so caught up in the never-ending cycles of archetypal
role-playing that we forget who is running the show. Do you even
realize how much of your energy goes down the drain like wasted
rainwater when you act like or try to become someone you are not?

The answer is "a lot." When people are put in a situation where
they know they are no longer in their element, they often feel like a

fish out of water. Do you think our ability to adapt and conquer comes with a price tag?

Pride can be good when it gives you the stamina to get up, when you are down. Unfortunately, pride can also be controlled by shame. Shame can keep you down for a long time. Pride will color your ego and polish it so your need to be noticed is recognized from miles away.

Unfortunately, this ego brightness is only temporary. It will only take you partway up the mountain you want everyone to know you are climbing. What you don't know, however, is there will be an experience waiting for you on this hike that is empowered by perfectly timed humility. That is where humility hits you with a four-by-four and you fall so far down, you may wake up next to Alice in Wonderland.

If all you do is act, but you think you are being true, you are likely surrounding yourself with individuals who are very similar to you. This is like having a dinner party and being served an exceptionally artificial meal on a plate of your own vanity.

What you do for a living is important. It will clarify where you belong in life. But if you let your career or title run your life, have you thought at least once about what else might be interfering with your life and probably running it, too? How many people do you know who identify themselves with their profession?

# # #

Be mindful about whatever you choose to do for a living. You don't have to try everything about a profession to understand how it is. Be a gentle and kind being. Use your common sense. The ripple effect of what you do can reach the shores of others' islands. You will have admirers and also enemies. But more important than having admirers is actually giving chances to your enemies, allowing them to see who you truly are.

So let's talk about some things that might benefit you, while you still live on this planet.

To begin with, you are not your identity. You are a being called "human." You are an energy form and magnetic. Some people are mindful, and some are not. Some are caring and thoughtful, but some are not.

Now, imagine a horizontal bar that stretches so far into infinity, we cannot possibly calculate its limits with our limited brain use.

Above that bar, put any thought, belief, or emotion that you consider to be positive. Then do the same thing for below the bar. There, list any thought, belief, or emotion you consider contrary.

While you do this, try not to see the positive as the ultimate goodness and the negative as the absolute evil. As you continue reading this book, you will come across the word "equanimity." It will introduce you to concept of "the middle way."

Pick a word for the space above the bar. Think of something that makes you feel good. How about *love*? What if there is a tug-of-war between the occupants above the bar and those below the bar? If so, what do you think the opponent of "love" above would be, below the bar?

Hate? Rage? What do you think? How about *fear*?

Love is connected to fear. What would you do in a situation where your loved one is in danger? Would you not cover them if the roof was falling? Would you not run back into the house for them, even if it was on fire? Would you not fight a dragon, if your loved one was in its path? Because love conquers fear, you would become the shield against any threat in order to defend the one you love.

Choose another word or idea on your own. Find its counterbalance in your reality, based on your data.

How about *anger*? When you feel anger, are you filled with bliss? Do you welcome the fire that anger manifests? Where would you place anger: above the bar or below the bar?

You will notice that any event will have a circumstance that produces a reason for the next thing to happen. **Anger can allow you to experience forgiveness, if you channel it without any attachments**. Anything can be channeled, for that matter. But, if you are attached to your ego, your point of view, and the pride defending that point of view, you can dull your senses.

Not only is what you think or say or how you choose to feel

important. So is what you do for a living. You get to decide what you do in any given moment. You can say, *"What about the relationship I feel suffocated being in, but I can't do anything about, because I have to protect my children?"*

This is a good example, I think. **There will be situations where you cannot really control anything other than the way you choose to perceive them.** It is like working for a company where you feel absolutely stuck in your job. You have options, and you can choose. Just remember that your choice is based on the condition created by your unsatisfied state of mind, created by your current job. Depending on what you do, new paths will open. Based on your choice, you will live in the flow of that particular action's energy current. However, the frequency of the new job may not be in harmony with your frequency of satisfaction. *Then* what are you going to do? Look for a new job?

Do you see how we can create cycles of disappointment?

- ❖ Mindfulness will be your key in your life. You do not have to rush into making any decisions. You really do not own the universe. Wouldn't that be just too much responsibility?
- ❖ Increase the number of kind words in your vocabulary.
- ❖ Extend your peripheral vision beyond what is available to see.
- ❖ Pay a compliment; it is free.
- ❖ Try to lift up someone's spirit.
- ❖ Don't just complete tasks in your daily life.

So what do you do for a living? Start with getting up, staying awake mindfully, and sharing the love in your heart. You can never know when it will be your time to ask for support. If you have a vision for a healthy life, make it bigger, so it can accommodate more of us.

Do not be stingy with your smile and with your love.
When you are asked what you do for a living, practice saying this.

"I share my light, even if it is with one being at a time. I stay awake. How about you?"

8

WELCOME TO WONDERLAND

SO, YOU OPEN YOUR eyes and start to get ready for your day. For many of us, almost every day is just like any other day. There is so much sameness.

You look at your childhood photo where you remember all the colors you carried in your heart. Then you look at yourself in the mirror, and all you see is gray. When you go out, you notice that not only has the world adopted the same gray color, but it has also chemically and artificially engineered different shades of gray. People are hypnotized by the variety of gray; to demonstrate their individuality, they become dissatisfied consumers. When they see one another, they offer compliments and flattery:

> *"Oh, my! Where did you get that shirt? I have never seen that shade of gray before."*

> *"Oh, this old thing? You should see the bathroom color I have just ordered. It is not yet available, but I put it on a layaway. It is called 'the gray with a touch of steel.'"*

> *"No! You mean steel as in the metal?"*

"Yes, indeed."

"You are so creative. This world needs more of you."

It is easy to get lost in our own reality, but we get upset when no one else seems to care about it. How do you recognize reality from within the collective? How do you wake up? How do you break down the walls of the studio where your life is being filmed? How do you stop cycles of stupidity? When do you find the courage to scrape the gray paint off your face so you can start to see the face of the abandoned child within you?

There may be a time when you are kicked out of your regular life. You may find you need to kiss goodbye to your comfort zone. You may lose your health or your relationship or your job or your friends or your possessions or all of it at once. What would you do if you did?

Would you stand up and say, "What a fantastic learning opportunity. Thank you, universe. I am so lucky. I am so blessed. Losing everything I had has never felt this good. Yeah!"

Or...

"Oh my! You know what? I am dead!"

Most of us will not be jumping up and down when we fall. We will not be overly excited about such an experience. On the contrary, we will likely close our wings shut, pull down the iron curtain, stop watering the flowers of our soul, and stop feeding the birds of our creativity. We will slowly tattoo our flesh with poison needles. We will close our eyes and have nightmares. We will be visited by angels of death-in-training to see if we are seriously considering taking our own lives so they can inform their boss.

When we fall, we don't see the wildflowers. The ground feels concrete. When we fall, we don't hear the canaries, only the laughing hyenas.

When we fall, first we need to notice *where* we land, instead of try to understand *why* we fell. When you look at the place you have just fallen, nothing may seem familiar to you. You may yearn for a familiar hand to lift you up, but you may have to learn to pull the open hand of yours and put it on your own heart, so its warmth will get your heart pumping blood through your life again and you can get up.

When you fall, take a deep breath first. And then another one. And another one.

Eventually, you will choose to get up, but you don't have to rush. You may feel like you are physically broken. Your hopes, dreams, faith, trust, and will to live may also seem broken, at first. The only thing that can actually break them, however, is the energy you put into it. **You have more power than anyone else, when it comes to destroying yourself**. If anything needs to be destroyed, destroy the identity you had when you fell.

In this experience, you will often question what is happening. You will want to know for sure what or if it is *really* going on. It will be difficult to believe. It will feel like you are watching someone else's life in a movie. But you will soon realize that it is actually happening to you. And your film will begin like this:

You wake up feeling nauseated. You don't recognize where you are. You hear people around you talking, but you do not understand them. Their lips are moving, but the words are not familiar to you. Then, one by one, they turn into racehorses. You may want to turn into one, too. But they take off as if they have missed a perfect opportunity, leaving you behind. Then, a helping hand takes you to a place where you share your loneliness with your own memories. If you want to be free and run like a wild horse, this is the moment that will defy you.

The first night after your fall will be cold. In your dreams, snakes will dance around your neck, bats will bite your toes, wolves will steal your courage, and the welcoming committee of the dark souls will visit you. Even the apple tree in your backyard will turn into an army of thorns, and its fruit will release the poison to feed your fear. You will toss and turn. You will wake up many times in your suffocating bed. Your sleepless first night will win the first round. And it will continue to win many of the subsequent nights, too.

You will receive many comments from the darkness. It will test your faith. You will hear its voice in your head telling you things like these:

➤ "Do you think this world will notice if you are not in it?"

➤ "Can you believe how many of your friends simply disappeared?"

➤ "After all you have done to support everyone, look how you are being treated now."

➤ "You have always helped others, but where are they now?"

➤ "If you end your life, maybe they will all realize what they have done to you."

➤ "You really don't deserve this."

➤ "Maybe your death will be a lesson to all."

➤ "You know your loved ones are not coming back to show their love to you anymore."

The darkness is a great salesman. It will sell your weakness back to you, wrapped in your own skin, and you will not even notice.

The darkness will turn on the television, and you will hear only disturbing news.

The darkness will change the frequency of your inner world to keep the light out.

So your test will be to decide if you choose to live or to leave it all behind.

When you choose life, the tree will turn green. Its fruit will release their nectar to feed you. Its leaves will cover you on cold nights. Its branches will grab the sunlight and deliver it to you. Your eyes will open up.

Welcome back!

Still, do not hurry to get up. This is the first day of your new life. You will have plenty of opportunities to stand up.

In Wonderland, your logic is irrelevant.

Rivers flow uphill, and the rain rises from the ground. The clouds will welcome your tears, and the sun will be underground.

When your life is upside down, your faith in yourself falls out of your heart and you linger amidst the confusion of the events in your life. In this circus filled with funny mirrors, you will not recognize yourself. Your disbelief about what is happening will spin fast everything about your suffering, but the pain you feel will still be in slow motion.

The answers you hope to get will be fed to pigeons in the park of your despair. The keys to your friends' houses will not open any doors to their paralyzed compassion. On the island of rejection, your memories will be your only blanket. But even that will not be warm enough to melt your sorrow. You will believe that your sadness is here to stay.

In Wonderland, you will learn to survive. You will meet new friends who will give you the keys to their houses. Every little step you take forward will teach you how to listen to the music of your heart. You will be tested and may even get very close to the edge of your sanity. Even then, despite the deceit you carry, you can still use your bare hands to start digging in the ground to unearth the sun.

The heaviness of your sorrow will re-establish normal gravity. You will look at the clouds and ask them to turn your tears to rain. You will touch the earth and tell it to grow flowers instead.

In Wonderland, where you live upside down; everything can turn around again. There is magic in such places. Anyone who finds himself falling into a hall and ending up in their own version of Wonderland will have access to the Book of Magic.

The Book of Magic's pages are filled with the stories of those who once were in your shoes. Each person has chosen to contribute their moment of waking up and finding their inner strength. At their own pace, many people have visited their own version of darkness, but not everyone has located the Book of Magic.

What would you write on the pages of your Book of Magic? How would you share your moment of awakening, when everything comes together in your life?

When you find yourself in Wonderland, do not try to find a way out too soon, or you may miss the point of being there. Do not rush, either. Sometimes, the bright light you need can be found on the wings of a tiny bug flying on the other side of the big wall you have built around yourself.

Healing is a journey. It will flow with its own current. When you are ready, you will step into the river of healing. Then, when the time comes for you to step out of it, your own land will be fantastic.

9

IN THE COMPANY OF TWO-WAY MIRRORS

YOU KNOW WHAT they say: There are two sides to every story.

This goes for you, too. Most people end up wasting a lot of time trying to prove their point of view. Even worse is trying to earn someone's love: trying to be noticed, not invisible or ignored; trying to be understood.

You cannot control the perception of others regarding how they choose to see you. Forget about it. Do not waste your time. Their caffeine consumption is not even relevant; no amount of it can keep them awake. Even if it seems like you all might be on the same train, it does not mean you all will get off at the same station.

In this life, while we think we mind our own business, we don't realize we actually are surrounded by two-way mirrors. Let's make this a bit more interesting and not so dry to digest.

You look in the mirror and see yourself. On the other side of the mirror, there is someone else who is also looking at you.

Can you guess who the person is on the other side of the mirror? That is you.

You have the ability to observe yourself. Most of us, however, do not get this correct. We, instead, judge ourselves and become our worst critic. The one on the other side can also have multiple alliances. Let's call those characters "archetypes." The character who will keep you down and invite more drama into your life when you fall is called "the victim."

Never give in to that character. Ever! The victim will steal the best possible version of your life from you and will make you skip the class that could be most beneficial to your happiness.

When you look at yourself in the mirror, the victim will beg you to lose yourself in the image. If you feel lost in the moment, any of the archetypes can take the opportunity to run your life for you. How are you going to claim your life back?

You will get yourself back through suffering. If you think you are worth it, you will learn to stitch up your own cuts with the needle you create from your tears. You will cry until your tears turn into rivers, hoping the oceans of the universe can hear you cry. Then, while you are sleeping, mermaids and dolphins will comfort you and kiss you goodnight. When you suffer, the light will not abandon you. The light-workers will come into your life; you don't even have to know who they are. You will do this one step at a time. And then, one day at a time.

However, the person who will save you is the child within you. All you need to do is look at yourself in the mirror without any judgment. Here is a clue: the child within is in your eyes. All it takes is enough courage to look at yourself in the mirror and see what *you* see, not what *others* see you as. You are not a by-product of others.

When you are in the presence of two-way mirrors, you need to hold onto the child within you. Most adults don't even remember where they left their child-self behind.

What was your reason for growing up so quickly?

When did you decide to ignore the child within you?

Are you even aware?

Take a look at children and then at adults. Surely you can see how different they are. The adult will spend a great deal of time trying to impress others.

Imagine a parent hearing her little daughter's voice saying,

"Look, Mommy. I got dressed all by myself."

One look at the little girl and the judge in you starts criticizing. You want to tell her your version of the truth. Now, would you tell that little girl what you *really* want to say? Would you *dare* tell her something like this?

"Oh, honey! What were you thinking? You are almost three years old and look at what you are wearing! First of all, everyone knows pink and red will clash. Daddy's shoes are not even in fashion anymore. Seriously, honey, you also carry a backpack? Unbelievable! If you think I am taking you anywhere looking like that, you are on your own. Here are the car keys. Go on, and drive yourself to your daycare."

How could you say that to a child? Would you?

Look at children, how they sing. Do you tell them to quit having fun as they continue to sing?

When they dance, do you break their spirits by telling them they have two left feet?

When they want to jump up and down in the living room, do you tell them to stop because they'll damage the carpet?

When they paint, do you make fun of them because their sun is bright yellow and there are always birds flying?

When they hug you for no reason, do you push them away and tell them you need your personal space?

When they get up to prepare you a surprise breakfast, do you yell at them because the toast is not perfectly golden brown?

When they feel under the weather, do you give them a hard time, saying, "Suck it up and get over yourself?"

When they pick the first rose of the season in the garden to give to you, do you hit them on the head with the flower and tell them you are so disappointed because that rose was not yet ready to be picked?

Is there a right time to show your love for someone?

Every adult was a child once. You know this very well. You would not treat a child unfairly like that, unless your heart is made of the coldest marble. Then why would you treat your adult self like that?

Why do you think that is? Why do we treat ourselves like that? Why do we allow others to treat us like that? Why? This life is a gift for you, and you have a right to open it. Do not let anyone tell you your gift is worthless. Until you get a chance to meet your true self, you will constantly run up and down escalators that take you nowhere, thinking you'll get to your destination faster than anyone else.

When you suffer, the child within you suffers, too. This is your opportunity to figure that out and then find ways to end your suffering.

You need to start by having a straight-from-the-heart, non-judgmental conversation with yourself. Yes, while you are looking at yourself in the mirror. You will not be alone in the company of a two-way mirror. Are you ready?

10

FALLING INTO THE RIVER OF OBLIVION

WE ARE CONVEYED into this life by floating on the river of oblivion. In this river, water plays multiple roles. First, it keeps you afloat, so you will be delivered. Second, it washes away all your knowledge and memories, so you don't have an unfair advantage over any other traveler. Third, it protects you from recruiters of both the darkness and the light, so you will have a fair start. Unfortunately, the river of oblivion's success rate is never one hundred percent.

So, what happens now?

First of all, not everyone makes it to this life. Second, some of us arrive with memories and knowledge from our previous place. Last, some of us come with a lifetime endorsement already provided by the darkness or the light. In many of our cases, it is from both of them. Otherwise, this planet would be very boring. Don't you think?

Our arrival is not a random act. It is planned, in part, with enough room left for synchronicity, coincidence, magic, and such. You get a kick-start right off the bat, but, just like anyone else, you find yourself in front of a fork in the road. Obstacles and choices, right?

Some will go to the left, and some will go to the right. Some will not move at all. Some will want to go back. Some will wait to be rescued from above. Some will be sucked underground. Some will wait, in case someone comes back from either direction, so they can ask them questions. Some will become remote viewers. Some will try to contact the recruiters who hover above the river of oblivion. Some will sell maps to confused travelers. And some will make their own pathway.

Which one are you?

What would you do?

How will you know what to choose?

In this life, you will always be making choices. This is not bad, as the alternative is other people making those decisions on your behalf.

Not every choice you will make will be the right one (or at least it will feel that way until you finally figure out it was right to begin with). Making a good choice requires wisdom, so you need to be awake. You cannot be sleepwalking and assume you will see what steps to take.

Every choice you make activates multiple possibilities for new experiences, so you are not off the hook yet! Let's take the fork in the road as an example. If you decide to choose one way, in the back of your mind you may wonder "what if?". Doubt acts like a double agent: while covering your back, it can also stab you in the heart. Being doubtful will cause you to linger and will steal your focus and commitment. And if you are not fully focused and committed, what will be the rate of return on your investment in life?

The universe will only match your contribution. So, whatever amount you choose to give, your focus and commitment to either the darkness or the light will be matched by the universe. What you invest in will grow.

Roads divide, going east and west, north and south, above, below, and anywhere in between. But at some point in your life, these roads will bring your path to cross with others. You will meet those who have been on different paths, not knowing if they walked into your life or if you walked into theirs. When that happens, take advantage of it. Act wisely, ask questions, but make sure you remain quiet when they answer. You really cannot hear much other than the sound of your own drum, when you talk. Learn to listen.

Everyone you encounter will have a gift to teach you. They will also have an opportunity to learn from you. Some people will be awake, but most will not. Those who are caught in the rat race are usually not awake. While you wonder about the roads you did not take, others will envy the roads you have taken. Most people will dream about what they don't have instead of being thankful for what they do have.

If you want to wake up, do not complain about the journey you have taken on the road of your choice. Instead, try to see what you have been offered. **Complaining will lower your calibration.** When your energy can no longer illuminate your desire to live, the darkness will get ahold of you. You will be swept off of your feet by a creature you think is Pegasus, but, in fact; you will be on the tusks of a serpent that has wings of wrath. Enjoy the ride!

If you want to wake up, your nightmares can also do that for you, but then they will become the reality of your daily life. Some of us set ourselves up for powerful, life-altering experiences wherein our south becomes the north. Then, the west becomes the east, above and below become sideways, and we wake up in the middle of a wolf pack feeling like a victim, because we think we are going to be torn into pieces, our blood dripping from the fangs of howling wolves.

When you find yourself in a situation like that, first of all you need to know you still have a choice. You can crawl into fetal position and let those who are ready to tear you to pieces like a pack of hungry wolves, or you can get up and turn things around by assessing your situation. Instead of becoming their delicatessen, you can choose to lead the pack.

11

LAMENTATION OF HYENAS

THERE WILL ALWAYS be a wolf pack around you. There will always be those who are ready to judge you, so you are only as good as your worst mistake. It is never easy to be judged by a friend: you feel abandoned by that person, when forced to face their unfair criticism. You will be disappointed to learn that the wolf pack is actually people you know. However, it will hurt you more when you finally understand that your so-called friends are not really on your side. Some will continue existing in your life, like ghosts from your past, and they will hold hands with those who have orchestrated the lamentation of hyenas all along.

Wake up! This time, make sure you are not only *looking* but that your eyes are indeed *seeing* the real faces behind the masks those people wear.

Although it is not easy to prove who is there for you, you don't want to be so foolish as to ignore their true faces, when they show them to you. But be careful: if you complain, then victimhood will take over. If you ignore them, you better remember the river of oblivion. If you don't choose, remember the fork in the road. Even if you think you are not doing anything, you are still doing *something*. Remember the cause and effect.

Some people may seem paralyzed when they witness your suffering. They may simply not know what to do. You may find them being stoic within their own limited reasoning. Some people may simply wait for you to ask them for help. Some may not have time for you, because they have their own dramas to attend to. Some may think you need to figure things out yourself. Some, however, will lend you a hand, while some will share their own light with you.

Meanwhile, some emotions such as anger, fear, deceit, grief, shame, humility, rage, stubbornness, and isolation will pull you into the darkness. The real magic occurs when you come back with the light to enlighten those who were so quick to judge you. If you hold grudge, however, you still have a lot of learning to do.

Collect your broken pieces, piece them together with your faith, and seal them with compassion. Sometimes, all we truly need is to fall apart and break into pieces, so we get a chance to see all our pieces in their own, self-contained places. Through those broken pieces and cracks, become the light you were meant to be.

Why do you think there are so many lonely people in the world? When it feels like your spirit is broken, does it mean the bridges between people are broken, too? How about those who stay together regardless of how many wars they have been through? What is it about the human spirit that can survive a fall from heavens but can easily be broken by a harsh word from a loved one?

Our strength travels between titanium and lace. Our emotions can visit the sky and also the burial grounds. Our thoughts can act like jugglers in the streets of our self-indulgence. We often get lost between the invitations from the lion's den and the crocodile swamp. We freeze with fears in our hearts.

Maybe some of us don't know how to share our sadness. Maybe some of us become sarcastic out of fear of being vulnerable. Maybe some of us use the wrong words and cut the heart of the one we love. Maybe our eyes are so intense and our look so stern so that they prevent others from seeing our tender hearts. Maybe we get good at pretending we are okay while we cover up our tears of sorrow.

What about lions? Do they also cry? Would you ignore a sad giant because you figure they are robust enough to heal their own wounds?

Do we rationalize leaving some people alone in their suffering because they have always been strong enough? Isn't that the easy way out? Isn't that a way of running away from our responsibilities—seeing someone who in need of help but choosing to turn our head away? If a healthy person falls into the fire, does he burn less than a weaker one? If the knife of deceit stabs him in the back, doesn't he bleed like the rest of us?

Have you ever witnessed a friend suffering who was also praised for handling it like a hero? Even so, was he still not a human?

The healing of a lion's broken heart is not any easier or faster than the healing of a mouse's broken heart. Although some of us might be better equipped, mentally, physically, emotionally and spiritually, our suffering is not *less*.

If a hyena cries, we may think he is laughing. But can we spend some time to understand what is actually happening? How do we know the seriousness of someone's sadness? Do we compare it to our own? Would that work?

We all have our own ways of lamenting. Some of us cry inside, so no one can hear us. Some of us make sure our pain is televised everywhere. Regardless of how you experience and reveal your suffering, if you know someone else is suffering, leave your analytical mind behind and take your compassionate heart with you. Ask if there is anything you can do, but don't rush to disappear if they reject your offer. Not everyone knows how to ask for and receive help. We all can use the help, however. And you know it.

12

BEING LEFT BEHIND AT THE TRAIN STATION

YOU DON'T REALLY know what just did happened, but you find yourself all alone at a remote train station. You then realize you got off at the wrong station and the train you were supposed to be on has already left. Your family, your friends, your job, your name, your dignity, and your reasons to live are all on the train.

Now what?

Oh, no! The hyenas are back! You feel so naked in front of them. Everyone is pointing their fingers at you and whispering. You know that they are saying about you…

"Look at him! Right there… Looking lost. Can you believe he got off the train right here?"

"Well, that's stupid."

"What was he thinking?"

"How is he going to catch up now?"

"No way!"

As a reader, you might be able to hear them, right? Maybe you even recognize that station. Perhaps, once, you got off at the same train at some point in your life.

What do you think a person might do? Jump in front of the next train and end this nonsensical drama because his life took off without him?

Start whining so, maybe, someone will help him? After all, the squeaky wheel gets the oil…

Wait there, because the train might come back?

Try to figure out what urged him to get off the train?

How come nobody stopped the train? Maybe he was not as important as he thought he was…

Maybe he was the biggest fool. Maybe his life was just a movie, and he was the star of his own show. Maybe he should *still* consider jumping in front of the next train…

# # #

What is the best thing to do when our life starts to suffocate us?

Breathe…

If you want to understand what happened, you need to be alive.

If you want to get back on the next train, you need to be alive.

If you want to start a new life where you got off the train, you need to be alive.

If you want to share your story and have it come out of your own mouth, you need to be alive.

Breathe…

You could also check yourself out. When we suffer, we are sometimes able to help others through our own journey, too.

The initial shock will not be washed away by the rain. Your initial sorrow will not be lifted away by sparrows. Your initial cut to the heart will not be put together by caterpillars. In fact, during this shock, you will likely be on your own. These are going to be hard times. If you are a survivor, however, life will not give up on you, either.

Breathe to stay alive. Breathe to reclaim your life. Breathe to share your life.

13

ATROCIOUS LEARNING

THIS TYPE OF LEARNING will not be served on a silver platter, garnished with mint leaf, poured over succulent berries. These lessons, instead, get delivered to you on the tongue of a beast of your choice. You cannot miss it. However, many of us are not even aware of what is being served. Welcome to the realm of being human.

Nobody will be served the exact same lesson. The lessons may look similar but are never the same. Just as everyone digests what they consume in their own personal way, some people will not be interested in these teachings; some people will overly analyze their ingredients; some people will want to trade theirs with others'; and some people will dig right in.

In this life, it is possible to find people who are very peaceful. They may never reveal they are enlightened. Even if they choose to remain discreet, their light still finds a way to shine. When you are around them, you may feel lighter. They are like the Earth, in a way. You can try to destroy it, but the Earth does not take it personally. Flowers still grow on it. The sun does not make sure every being gets its warmth; we just know it is there. These people have learned, perhaps in a harsh way, not to take things personally.

If you compare your lesson to someone else's, your learning is still ongoing. If you think you have suffered more than others, your education is still in progress. Leave everyone else's story alone, and focus on your own. You may need some serious time to learn your own lesson.

You better start becoming your own best friend. **The only relationship you should be more concerned about is the one with your child-self.** If you can ask the child for help, you will not be denied. If you are a good student, these lessons will be embedded in you. Many wonderful experiences will merge to teach you about the following and many more:

Compassion: No lesson is complete without it. This is when you know you are no better than any other being. Compassion will teach you to release your ego and need for self-centeredness. You will notice we are in this together. You will learn to help others. You will learn to share and give. When you help others, you will also benefit. When you lift others up, you will also lift yourself.

No judging: You will learn not to judge anymore. You will no longer assume things, either. You will see that humans are both simple and complicated. Their story may not be as deep as yours, but you cannot know how many more stories or sub-stories they have. We all make mistakes. If they are ready to learn from you, then you will be their teacher. If they are not willing to learn from you, then they are not your students. You cannot teach those who are not yet ready. Do not judge anyone. Do not judge yourself.

Listening: You will listen more and talk less. By having compassion and being non-judgmental, you will accept the fact that we are no different than one another. So let them speak their words, if they have a need to judge or criticize you. You do not have to defend yourself. Just let them speak. When they realize you are listening, you will begin to gain their trust. But listen with sincerity, respect, and all your senses, not just with your ears.

Loneliness: This one is not so easy to absorb. When you suffer, you are alone in your journey, even when you are surrounded by many people who are truly empathic about your situation. You will feel the chilling loneliness in your bones. Do you think loneliness can be shared? If it can, then should it still be called loneliness? It can be shared with nature. The trees will listen to you. The birds will still land next to you. You can share it with the walls. You can turn your sadness into graffiti and color it in any way you want. You know what, though? Nothing is permanent. Your loneliness will also pass. Be patient.

Patience: You knew this was coming, right? Next time, observe those who are calm and patient. Ask them, if you dare. You will find out that suffering teaches you to be more patient. When you suffer, life does not move fast. You'll notice how yours moves in slow motion. While the pain feels like it lingers, agonizingly slow, you will notice every dust particle in the air you breathe. You cannot rush life's teachings. You cannot skip its chapters. If you try to skip, you will be asked a question about the very section you have omitted! You cannot get away from it. So be patient and read each page carefully without prejudice.

Endurance: The second you give up, your learning experience will pause indefinitely until you decide to push the activate button. If you enable your endurance instead of giving up, you have a greater chance of standing up to see what your future holds. Endurance will be your personal trainer during the marathon of your life. It may feel like you are being pushed to run uphill, but when you finally reach the top, you will be able to see all the places you have been. You will realize you are standing exactly where you are supposed to be. Do not give up.

Calmness: If you are not calm, then you are not focused. If you are not focused, then you are distracted. If you are distracted, then you are not in the moment. If you are not in the moment, then you are sleepwalking. If you are sleepwalking, then you are not awake. If you are not awake, then you will miss the whole lesson. It is your choice. You can multitask and be proud of it, or you can focus on one thing at a time, take one step at a time, and be calm. Calmness is your ticket to a safe place where you do not have to hurry up to make stupid decisions.

Sincerity: You will learn not to be pretentious. Really, do not be fake! You know it, everyone else knows it; even their dogs know you are fake, too. Your sincerity level will increase once you experience humility. When you are not sincere, how can you be true? Is it even possible? Sincerity comes with being humble. You will learn that everything you give redounds to your sincerity and authenticity. It comes back to you sometimes directly and sometimes indirectly. So, be sincere, give sincerely, and live sincerely. It will bring you closer to your true self.

Humility: This is a great experience to have, since nothing else can kick you in the rear end of your pride. Humility will strip your stage clothes off. Humility will remove your badges, tattoos, and medals. Humility will melt your masks. It will teach you that anyone can fall. It will remind you that we all can make mistakes. Humility will not recognize any gender or skin color. When it is your time, you cannot run away from this experience. You will learn that the pride that has been feeding your ego can easily run out of steam. Your nakedness can become the warmest fabric in the cold winters of gaining wisdom.

Kindness: When you suffer, you need support. Even though it is your own lonely journey, you still will need support. Those who are kind at heart will support you and at least keep you afloat. Kindness is contagious. It will find its residence in your heart at first contact. Then, it will move into others'. It is the true form of paying it forward. You will remember someone else's kindness toward you, and, most likely, you will do the same for others. Your kind heart will attract those who need kindness, and you will not turn them away.

Truth: It is possible that everyone has their own version of truth. But when it comes to your own, you cannot fool yourself all the time. You will learn the truth about yourself: what you are made of, your limits, your strengths, and your weaknesses. You will be free.

14

OVERLOOKING VERACITY

WE DO IGNORE truth sometimes, don't we? But why?

When we are in the river of oblivion, we really do not know where the flow will take us to. The completion of that journey brings us to this life. The average length of a journey to this earth as a human being is around nine months or so. However, we are exposed to many solicitors while in the river, when we don't yet know much about anything.

The river branches off into millions of tributaries that spread across the planet. Your river will take you to your mother. Through her, you will be downloaded a lot of information. Your mother is also exposed to so many solicitors, just as you are. There is a strong possibility she will not be able to filter everything, and you, as a baby in her tummy, will receive some of that information. Your mother's love is stronger than her fear, yet you will receive both feelings.

During your journey on the river, there will be moments when you flashback to your previous place. You will also be reminded of other travelers in other branches of the river of oblivion. You will be told that this is for your information only, but, in your human life, you will cross paths with some of those travelers.

Of course, you will not remember this, once you are born. The darkness will tell you it is okay to cut corners. The light will tell you to become wise. You will download an incredible amount of data, as though you were constantly be watching hundreds of television channels. However, since your conscious mind can only store so much data, most of this information will be dumped into your subconscious mind. It will be your homework to tap into your subconscious mind and pull out the information you need. Good luck with that! It is like trying to find your contact lens at the bottom of an ocean. You can do it, right?

Do not worry too much, because your reactions and responses, based on how you are triggered by who knows what, will activate certain signals in your subconscious mind so that very specific piece of information will rise to the conscious level. And when that happens, you will say, "I have no idea why I did that... I really don't know why that person makes me feel unsafe... I don't know why I reacted like that... I didn't mean to say that... I don't know what came over me... Oh, my! This feels like déjà vu... I feel like I know you from somewhere..."

You get the picture, right?

So, when we are not true to ourselves, does it mean we are being controlled by something else? How do we reach the point to be able to say *this* is what I want to be when I grow up?

Are we always conscious, when we make decisions? If we are not, then isn't it like driving with your eyes closed? That can't possibly be safe for anyone, yet we still do things not knowing or understanding why.

What if we have no clue about our true self? How do we even start revealing that? How do we tell the truth, distinct from its spurious entourage?

Your senses may not be enough to help you become enlightened, unless they are utilized together. They need to be united. This usually does not happen, as humans become very comfortable relying on one source only. So, what you think you saw or what you think you heard or what you think you tasted or what you think you touched or what you think you smelled and what you thought—these could perfectly be fine for you to use, to base your decision on. If we only knew how dysfunctional beliefs are created, we would always take a deep breath first, and then think again before we act.

This is how the spine of your identity is created: simply by relying on your senses. Nothing will look the same, if you look at it from different directions. Your perception could be duplicitous, and your unbending pride could be a bewitching dance partner. Together, their dance would burn the floor of your trust, and your credibility would burn to the ground along with it.

Do not be so silly as to put all of your eggs in the fragile basket of your senses. They can be tricky. The reality you are in could make you think it is all about you. But if you choose to see, multiple realities are happening simultaneously. This synchronous illusion of life becomes orchestrated magnificently. And we think the music is playing only to our ears. This is the identity you have, and you think you were born with it. You, the mastermind of chaos, have indeed engineered your identity blindly.

If you can engineer your identity, what else do you think you can engineer? What if your identity decides to multiply itself by splitting itself into different characters? Or even into multiple personalities? Could we be overlooking veracity because of our inner characters, perhaps?

It seems like the concept of truth has been personalized by many of us. While you have *your* version of it, your dance partner has *his* version of it. Is this one way to overcome our boredom? Do we create identities and stories to manifest their existence?

Traveling between different thoughts, being exposed to many different emotions, and having to make many decisions in life somehow take its toll on us. We sometimes feel like doing nothing. In fact, there are people out there who are doing nothing with their lives. They are content with whomever they think they are and whatever they think they are doing. They do not get up with a spark. They get up so they can go back to bed at some point. They are like hamsters in a wheel: as long as it is turning, they do not mind repeating the same cycle again and again.

The secret to being true to yourself is not locked, sacred, in the safe of someone else's perception of you. It is written in a language that can only be decoded by being exposed to your DNA. No one else has the same code. No one else has the same blueprint. So, how are you going to decode what your truth is?

It is not that difficult to do, if you pay attention to the thoughts and feelings that visit you. However, you have to learn to accept they are not permanent. In fact, everything is impermanent.

Remember that: everything changes. Some things change faster than others. When nothing is permanent, can you accept that feelings and thoughts are not there to stay? Here is the part that will determine how close you are to decoding your blueprint. It seems like, when the body and the mind agree on something, when there is no resistance from either side, we believe we are doing the right thing. Like when we eat a healthy food: your body feels good, because it knows the food you are consuming is healthy. Your mind makes the statement you have learned along the way: "*It is good for us to eat an apple a day.*" So, you feel good. You are doing the right thing.

Let's turn this around. You feel a bit down, and you crave ice cream. Your mind says, "*You know, so what? Just a little bit of it will not damage anything.*"

Then you consume some and then some more. Your stomach says, "*Oh, no! I am going to be sick. Stop! No more!*"

You, on the other hand, continue to eat more because your mind keeps telling you, "*Good for you. Don't be too rigid. You have a right to eat something unhealthy every now and then. So what?*" It looks like your mind and body are not aligned.

The other factor that should be in this picture is your heart. Imagine a triangle between your mind, body, and heart. When the mind is absent, it ping-pongs between the darkness and the light. Mindfulness grounds you and connects the mind to your heart by keeping it within the body.

If this is so, then where do feelings come from? How do we know they are not products of the mind? Could our mind be a double agent? How do we know what we feel is real? What about thoughts? Are we the creator of our thoughts?

If the mind and the body are not aligned, you better start paying attention to them. If your gut is telling you something when your mind tells you something else, do you think your heart will become the final decision-maker? Has your heart ever been wrong before?

Then how do we find our true self? Do we travel the entire universe? Do we ask the galaxy?

What if we were to stop acting? So many of us act, right? How about you? Sometimes, you say you have a favorite color and share it with your friends. Do they overly analyze your choice of favorite color? Do you feel like you have to prove *why* you love that color? Let's hope your answer is no.

Think about the people and things in your life. You do not have to prove why you love someone or something. Love should not require proof. If the emotion in your body feels authentic and your mind does not fight against it, would it be reasonable to say what is happening to you is not fake? If something is not fake, would it be correct to say that it must be real?

Nobody has the ability to know anyone else's true self. However, some people think they are entitled to share their thoughts on that delicate subject, for some reason.

So, do not think about the collective version of the truth for a minute. Focus on yourself. What does it mean to you? Imagine a situation where you are doing something you dislike but feel you have to do. What is telling you to pursue that? Why do you proceed? Is it your mind? Is it your body? Is it your heart? If it is your guilt telling you to do whatever it is, was the feeling of guilt initiated by your mind or by your body? Where did the feeling of guilt come from?

The sense of guilt can come either from the darkness or the light. It is not really *within*, because you are a transparent, energetic being. So, it is not generated on the inside. You do not give birth to the "feeling of guilt"; it is generated outside of you. Feelings are available for all of us. They existed before our arrival and in their own realm. They are like air molecules and cannot be purchased by any of us. So, why would you hold on to an air molecule and announce to the world it is yours? It was out there before you, but now you think you captured it, so now it is yours?

Why would you take ownership of the emotion "feeling guilty"? Perhaps something triggers your mind and body, like you are a runway at the airport, and your mind receives a request for an emergency landing. So, "feeling guilty" is the plane. Where does it land? If you allow it to land in the first place, why should you not release it, so it can take off? How many planes do you think you can store on your limited runway?

Ask yourself if it feels natural to you. If you hesitate in your answer, your internal compass is warning you. Yes, **we all have an internal compass**. Do you use yours?

15

THE LABYRINTH OF YOUR IDENTITY

THE REALM WHERE ALL versions of you linger is nothing but a labyrinth. Unfortunately, some of us reside in this place and continue to play a game of hide-and-seek.

You may not find what you are looking for, if you don't know where you are going. When all the walls in your environment look the same, you may not remember where you have been. Being lost might be an opportunity for some, but also the end of the line for many others.

There is only one way for you to find the exit out of the labyrinth you have created: by changing things. If the roads you linger on do not take you to the places you want to go, then you need to figure out how to rise above to discover other routes.

To rise above, you have to let go of the extra weight you have been carrying. You need to be light.

Most of the weight we carry—and we don't even know why— was gained when we ignored messages sent through our emotional pandemonium. **There are signs around us all the time**. When we are ready to see them, the signs become visible. These emotions have already signed contracts with your mind. However, when your mind acts like a gatekeeper, it can trick you into ignoring some emotions. These neglected emotions will manifest physical symptoms in order to get noticed, including nausea, pain, anxiety, digestive problems, numbness, irritability, loss of senses, and much more. How do you terminate the contract signed between the emotions and the mind? More important, how do you terminate the power of the mind over your body and spirit?

So, how do you rise above?

Rising above requires a shift in your frequency. That starts with your thoughts. You really need to change the way you choose to perceive some things in your reality. Changing the frequency of your being is a process that should not be taken for granted. It will require your full commitment, and, if you choose to be evasive, you will only continue fooling yourself. So make a commitment. Be an excellent student.

Your frequency has its own language, just like the billions of others' on this planet. It also has multiple components and ways of being delivered. This means, to get along with someone else on a particular topic, you both need to be traveling within the same frequency.

Imagine purchasing a seat on a specific flight to a specific city and someone buys a ticket for the seat right next to you. Now watch out! This does not mean you are soul mates instantly. It only means that your paths have crossed at that specific time. Do you remember the river of oblivion? Even when we travel on different rivers, our paths can still cross. While you sit next to each other, you do not have to share your life stories to figure out if this was arranged cosmically. Perhaps the sign you need to see is visual, such as their tattoo or necklace or the book they are reading. You cannot and should not push it, because it will not reveal itself to you until you are ready to see it.

How do you change the frequency of your livelihood then?

Imagine you have a job that you are not happy doing. You force yourself out of bed in the morning. Your stomach aches. Traffic looks so uninviting. One of your co-workers drives you crazy. What you do is not fulfilling, but it pays the bills. You simply do not want this job, but it feels like you have no other choice.

First if all, you *always* have a choice. Now, just to be practical, let's give a number to the frequency of your state of mind every time you think about your job. Let's say that number is fifty-three.

The energetic message vibrated out of your fifty-three frequency level will only have so many privileges. It is like being on a cruise ship. Depending on your finances, you book a certain cabin on that ship. Let's say your fifty-three is equivalent to one of the rooms on the lower floors and does not come with windows, because it is actually below the waterline. You do not like your room, because you wanted to have a window. They tell you, if you want to book one of the higher rooms, where you can see the dolphins swimming next to your window, you need to pay extra. In your case, your frequency level has to be *more* than fifty-three, so you cannot afford to book a nicer room with a view at that time.

At work, the co-worker who drives you crazy is actually a great gal: everyone indeed likes her, and she is very popular among her peers. Her frequency is more than fifty-three. You may try to act like her or dress like her, to see whether you might create similar attraction. But because your commitment to the shift you want to make is not one hundred percent, your attempts will not succeed.

Do you remember the section about how needing accurate data or a correct record in your subconscious mind is like trying to find your contact lens at the bottom of an ocean? Good. Because your chances of figuring out why you really do not like that gal are as close as it gets to finding your contact lens. However, it is never impossible.

Let's do this. Are you ready? Yes, we are heading toward a beautiful but slightly painful journey into the different levels of your subconscious mind. Here is your first tip: *Relax!* Because, if you are not relaxed, you cannot get into the subconscious mind. Being relaxed is like your access pass to the subconscious mind, so use it wisely by staying calm. Here is another tip: Go back to your childhood first and perhaps even further beyond it.

If you are fully committed, then, however long it may take, you will always find out why you do not like your popular co-worker. Consider trying this: Write down what you don't like about that person. Okay, perhaps you write down twenty things. Make sure you are being honest. Write down *everything,* even if it is about her golden locks or fingernails.

Okay, after you think more about it, you note down her teeth, name, sense of fashion, her laugh, and so on. You probably have forty things on your list that you do not like about this person. Good. The first part of your homework is done. Take a break. Drink some chamomile tea. Relax.

Your next steps all require your honesty, sincerity, and being genuine and connected to yourself.

Start reading each item on that list out loud. Make sure you do this in private. Once you have gone through the list, say this to yourself:

"I am going to read the list again, but this time, I want my body to respond to me by giving me a physical signal to let me know which one of these items I should pay closer attention to."

You may not be able to sense it easily in your first attempt, but do not give up. Do it again. Say the word and wait for your body's response. Do it again. Do not give up because, eventually, you will hear what your body is telling you.

Let's say that when you repeat the word "*social*" you get a tiny cramp in your stomach, but you ignore it because you can't possibly see how that could be the signal. So what? You do it again, and this time the cramp feels stronger when you repeat the word "*social*."

Take a break, and take a deep breath.

It is now high time to dissect the word "social."

So, what does it mean? Why would your stomach react to the word "social"?

Let's talk about "muscle memory" for a bit. In some of the earlier pages, under the chapter named "Touching the Needle of the Spinning Wheel," I mentioned two important messages you would be given before your arrival in this world:

❖ Collect data while you are there. Do not forget when someone tells you something you have never heard before. Record it. Make sure the data is not breached. Collect data.

❖   You are not the data you collected.

In your case, the statements above have worked like this:

The word "social" was used to describe you, but not in empowering way. It was the first time you heard it in such a negative sense, and you recorded it, not knowing if it was an accurate way to define you. You simply collected the data.

Unfortunately, you also became the data you collected.

Now, how in the world are you going to remember *who* the heck it was who used the word "social" toward you in such a way that it hurt your stomach badly, but you chose to sleepwalk instead of bury that incident at the bottom of your subconscious mind?

I did not say this would be easy to figure out. While you work on this one, guess who is going to visit you?

You will hear a knock on the thick walls of your confused state of mind. You will open the door to see a little girl selling cookies for her school. She says, "Ma'am, please buy a box of cookies. This is a very special cause. It is a 'social' study we were to complete for our school. Please, ma'am, would you please buy one?"

You buy one, of course, and she leaves your sight so happy. While you watch her leave, you notice a feather fly out of her hair and land on your doorstep. You pick up the feather, not really understanding what is happening. You go back inside and put the box of cookies on the table with the feather next to it. However, you still don't put the two together, because your frequency still lingers at fifty-three. You go to sleep that night, but you can't fall asleep because something is bothering you. You feel restless and somehow disappointed, because you have no idea that you were triggered by the word "social" and didn't even know it. You are about to give up.

Who do you think interferes with you, when you are ready to give up?

So, you still are restless and cannot fall asleep. You decide to pass the time by distracting yourself. You turn on the television, where the breaking news is on. They are talking about an epidemic caused by certain type of Girl Scout cookies sold in a specific region of the country. After that news, you naturally do not want to take a chance, so you toss the box of cookies into the trash. As soon as you leave the room, the reporter on television bursts out laughing behind your back and yells, "Sucker!" But you do not hear.

After taking out the trash, you come back inside and start to get ready for bed again. You hear a noise outside. Instead of getting into your bed, you turn on the porch light and discover a raccoon helping himself to your trash. He disappears as soon as he sees you, and you grudgingly start to clean up the mess he's made. You put all the trash back in the bin. On your way back to the house, you step on something. You look down and see the box of unopened cookies. You pick it up but don't understand why the raccoon would not even touch them.

You notice something written on the box that hadn't caught your eye before. It says: *Social introverts are the silent cheerleaders.*

Bingo!

Your heart starts to pound. Pay attention to this one, as it is a muscle memory at work. Your stomach muscles remember something. You know something feels different this time. You keep thinking about that sentence, as you know something about it has somehow slapped you in the face.

In the morning, you go to work. Something still feels different, and you do not notice the traffic. You are not bothered by it. Your frequency goes up to fifty-five. You arrive at work and the first person who says good morning to you is the person of your nightmares. You cannot believe she actually noticed you! You pull yourself together and say, "Good morning" back to her. Your frequency is now at sixty.

A week later, the gal of your nightmares invites you to lunch. Still in disbelief, you accept her invitation. During lunch, she wants to know why you never join the rest of the team during breaks, etc. You politely explain that such things are not really your cup of tea. Your co-worker, however, does not buy that. Then you share that you consider yourself an introvert. *Oops!* Your frequency just went down to fifty-nine.

When she tells you she was actually just like you when she was a teenager, you cannot hide your surprise. She tells you a story about how lonely she felt when her family moved into a different school district and how she did not have any friends. All the cheerleaders, however, had many friends. She then says one of her teachers told her that the **limitations we think we have are actually nothing but opportunities to find out what we are made of**. Therefore, she should never label herself introvert or extrovert, social or not. Her teacher also reminded her that she can be whatever she chooses to be. Even a cheerleader, if she wants. However, she should not become one if she thinks that is the only way for her to have friends.

A tear falls down on your cheek. She asks if you are okay. You tell her you have never been better, even with tears in your eyes.

That evening, once you are home, you add one more word to your list. It is the word "cheerleader." You read the word out loud. Your heart starts to pound, your lips tremble, and you start to cry. You remember the day you were at cheerleading tryouts and were not chosen because they said you were not social enough. With that recollection, your frequency rises to one hundred; you just released one of your dysfunctional identities. You notice an opening in the walls of your insecurities labyrinth. You no longer feel stuck.

# # #

This, of course, was a simple example. Most of us linger in this life by keeping ourselves busy and not noticing the signs. **If you want to meet your true self, start by detaching yourself from the identity you have been holding onto**. You will see the connection between the events taking place in your life and those who are in them. As a result of this awakening, who knows? Maybe someday you will help someone else to shed their identity.

Your frequency will change…

> ➢ When you turn your dysfunctional belief into a functional one
> ➢ When you no longer expect anything in return
> ➢ When you truly give
> ➢ When you are happy and thankful for your own company

- ➢ When you no longer have the need to prove
- ➢ When you sincerely help others
- ➢ When you accept what is happening and the way the things are
- ➢ When you no longer blame
- ➢ When you are tolerant and compassionate
- ➢ When you are wiser...

And when it does, your place in this life will also change. Those who cannot connect to your frequency will have to go.

And your loneliness will become your teacher, showing you how to love yourself. Everything changes and nothing is permanent.

16

PERPETUAL SORROW

THIS TYPE OF SORROW is actually transient, but it cuts our hearts so deeply, we lose our faith and believe nothing can restore it. Others may tell us the sun will rise again the next day, but, when we feel buried in our sadness, we believe the sun will not show up to light our darkness.

Life serves its lessons to us in many unimaginable ways. However, we seem to have been programmed to focus only on our own sorrow. We ignore the fact that suffering is indeed for everyone. Any level of entrapment in any kind of sorrow can steal a great deal from you. It can keep you chained to the pole of drama. You can become so numb that hurricanes and earthquakes won't make you move. It can feel like your spirit is soaked in muddy water and has been for so long that you forget how to laugh. Sorrow visits every bone in your body every time you breathe.

When you feel broken, you may not be interested in hearing other people's happy songs. However, sorrow is just a stopover during your journey to compassion. Your aching heart will continue to beat, and you will continue disbelieving.

Isn't it amazing sometimes how we cannot recognize the

strength we've had all along? We cannot comprehend how we survive through such sadness. When does that strength come into the picture? Is there something else in control, so we die at the right time, according to divine plan? Do we benefit from experiencing sorrow at all? Or does sorrow destroy it all?

Sorrow is the absence of joy, just like the dark is the absence of light. So, joy is there all along, even when all you feel is sadness. But how can you even consider the possibility of seeing the light when you feel like you are fighting for your life, trying to survive in the dark? How do you reach the other end of the tunnel?

Sorrow is like the lotus flower: its life starts in the dark and muddy bottom of a pond. Such a beautiful flower is born out of the darkness, as if rising from the ashes. Sorrow is like that pond: it can provide you the nutrition to grow and transform yourself, so your truth starts to blossom. But its heat may burn you and dry the blood in your veins. You may feel dehydrated. Your heart may feel weak, pumping the ghost of your blood out of dry veins.

Sorrow does not require an appointment to knock on your door. Do not assume it sucks the life out of you, alone. Your constant sorrow can blow out the candles of other loving souls around you, as well. How do you think they get their flame back? Is there a supply of fire where we can all get our flame back?

There is enough joy stored in this life for all of us. Nobody will return empty-handed, if they need help graduating from losing themselves in sorrow. Everyone will be lifted up, if they are ready to spread the ashes of their sorrow.

You cannot bury your sorrow and count on visiting it someday. Your sorrow is not there to take over your life. It is not there to steal your breath or consume your happiness. Sorrow will visit your life for a reason. It will be activated for a reason. You will eventually find out the reason for your cries. But how are you going to see those reasons when your eyes are filled with tears all the time? How are you going to understand the reasons when your mind is trapped in the cobwebs of confusion? How do you accept those reasons when it feels too late for them to become apparent to your heart? How will you trust the accuracy of those reasons when it feels like your hope is no longer? Where can you go when it feels like your feet are buried in a concrete block?

Moving forward with so much pain in your heart is not easy because it feels so heavy. You may start to believe that you are losing hope when all you experience is sadness. You notice you find temporary comfort in the company of your own loneliness. You feed the loneliness with your sorrow, and, in return, the sorrow keeps you in its custody. You pull down the curtains, stop taking showers, and avoid mirrors. Sorrow moves into your house and starts changing the colors on your walls and covering your furniture with fabric of the darkness. It teaches and trains you so well, you no longer have any need to feel the sunshine in your bones.

However, sorrow has two sides. Depending on which side you are willing to see, you will either sign a contract to go down with it or you will learn to rise above it. As long as you know that sorrow is not permanent, you may find a reason in your heart to believe you can go through such a journey because the destination is worth it. When you listen to sad songs, when you recognize the sadness in a stranger's eyes, and when your sorrow brings you closer to those who are less fortunate than you are, you may take a chance and introduce yourself to the other side of sorrow.

Sorrow is like unwanted crows invading your cornfield, completely ignoring the scarecrow of your soul. You don't know how to get rid of them. You chase after them, you throw rocks at them, and you even stay up all night to yell at them. However, the fear invades you. What if the crows are there to stay?

Then, one day, you decide to listen to them instead of chase after them. You start to hear their song. You realize they are not after your harvest. They are there to teach you. You stand still. The rain has stopped. It is cold outside, but your curiosity keeps you warm. Then, coyotes approach you from the depths of the fields. This is the first time you have had enough courage to face what has been bothering you.

Sorrow is a message sent to you by your child-self so you can feel what the child needs. Even if it is an hour spent in an amusement park, dreaming of winning a stuffed animal, your child-self will not forget what he wanted and never got.

Look your sorrow in the face and ask, "Why am I so sad?" Sadness will also change your frequency. It will take you to people and places where you may experience things that can actually cause you to wake up. It will drive you through different emotions, resurrected by memories, where you may have to meet your fears encouraged by your demons.

If you do your homework and are wise, you will soon realize that sorrow is nothing but a great teacher helping you to love and be kind and compassionate. **When you understand the reason for your sadness, you may realize you no longer need to cling to it.** When you release the sadness, in the same way that the dark disappears with the arrival of the light, joy will find its place in your heart.

So do not be an enemy of your sorrow. Do not ignore it or pretend it has no mission. Your sorrow *does* have a mission: to teach a few things.

- ❖ Cut yourself open so you see what is inside.
- ❖ Allow yourself to see all those around you who have scars.
- ❖ Let them show you how they have learned to live with those scars.
- ❖ Stitch your cuts with love.
- ❖ Notice how the scars disappear in the heart of the child within.
- ❖ Tell and show others what you have learned.
- ❖ Take the child to an amusement park of his choice.

Just like any other challenging experience, sorrow is also there to show you how to obtain wisdom. Because, without wisdom, there will always be crows and coyotes in your life. **Without wisdom, the amazing experience of sorrow will be nothing but a wasted opportunity for a person unwilling to wake up.**

17

WHO IS YOUR DANCE PARTNER?

WHO IS YOUR dance partner? Is it fear or love? Is it revenge or forgiveness? Is it hatred or compassion? Who is it? What is it?

You and your dance partner's intention and choice of music will determine how you perform. So, do you have a dance partner, or do you think you dance alone?

We all have multiple dance partners, even if we are not aware of it. Your dance partner lives within you and instructs you how to move. Your life can be the way you choose to live, but, if you are not awake, your life will be lived the way your dance partner sets it up for you. Many of us dance to music that is chosen for us. When we continue to dance with our eyes closed, what do you think we might not be seeing? You have the option to stop this nonsense, if you want to. However, that will not be easy when your moves are controlled by your dance partner. The only way to stop is by looking your dance partner in the eyes. There you will see you are dancing with yourself.

You are indeed your dance partner. Your conscious and subconscious minds are partnered to use your existence to move through the rhythm of life. Some of us feel awkward; some of us stumble and perhaps even freeze on the dance floor.

Looking your dance partner in the eye requires courage. The ability to do is strengthened when you find yourself on the path of suffering. Walking on an unfamiliar road will introduce "fear" as your dance partner.

Fear, like any other state of mind where thoughts and emotions are fabricated, can be used to your advantage or it can reinforce victimhood and continue to feed your suffering. Fear is like an ice storm. You can barely breathe and barely hear your own heartbeat. When fear paralyzes you, can you even dare to move?

Once fear hacks into your system, it delivers a virus to all of your programs. You start to slow down and may even suffer from memory loss. You start to lose your capacity to operate. In the narrow passages of hopelessness, you will start to suffocate. Fear will turn off the lights in the channels of your catacomb. It will bury you in your own depression, and your mummified glimpse of life will gradually fade and dry like a rose in winter.

If you give in, then fear will take everything you have. Although it is after your faith and soul, once you are in the garden of hopelessness, fear will not water your flowers. Like so many others before you, you will start to dig deeper in the dirt, believing perhaps the suffering will end if the earth just opens up and swallows you.

Because you think you cannot see in the dark, would you be willing to give up believing in the fact that the light does exist?

Remember, **fear is just a transient trespasser.** Would you prefer if that intruder moved in with you? If it moves in with you, it will tell you that the storm of the century is heading your way. And you better shut all the windows, pull down the curtains, and seal the shutters from outside, too.

It will exhaust the oxygen supply to your brain, and you will slowly stop thinking clearly. When you start to make no sense, you know you will become your number-one fan. The show you put on will only be applauded by your own confused hands.

By then, the fear will own your house. In your own home, you will become a stranger. You will drift away on the seas of the unknown. On this journey, however, you may realize there is always a possible way to reclaim your home.

Go back and get it.

How?

Sit down and have a chat with the fear.

Ask, "Why did I invite you?"

"How did you trick me?"

"What is the reason you chose me?"

It is okay to ask. Go ahead and ask.

When you recognize the courage you already have, it will activate your immune system to act as an antivirus program on your computer. You will start the cleansing process. This catharsis of your residency in oblivion will wash the dirt off you. It will lift you up and you will stop turning into the pillars of your own mausoleum.

We all have access to fear. If the fear visits you, it is okay to acknowledge it, as there is a reason for its visit. However, you do not have to give up your seat in this life.

You need wisdom to see what the fear is trying to teach you. Do not ignore it, but do not offer it a permanent residence in your body, either.

Be aware of its moment of entry into your body. Study the area of your body where the fear resides. It is important to know where you sense fear in your body. That region of your body will pulsate because your body has its own grid lines where energy travels.

Remember, **we are energetic beings**. Therefore, for fear to survive, it will need your energy. Like a vampire in the night, fear will suck your hope dry while you continue to sleepwalk.

Is it time for you to wake up?

18

VANADIUM OF VENGEANCE

VANADIUM OF VENGEANCE is like chasing a shooting star down to the bottom of an abyss. It will only harden your heart's ability to have compassion. It is not worth it. Any form of vengeance is a trip to the land of nothingness, and you will return empty-handed from that lonely journey. Do not purchase that ticket. It is a scam.

Vengeance is false reasoning created by the Human Resources Department of the darkness, which promises you a position as the future president of a non-existant company.

The reward of any vengeance is a temporary victory built on the dunes of your regret. The shackles you put on the ghosts are nothing but your own.

Do not chase after trains you can never catch. Instead, find another way to get there. Instead, find another train, one operated by understanding, kindness, and compassion.

Every time you think you are getting even with someone, you are actually becoming uneven with yourself. Every time you waste your precious energy to get even with someone, you actually are stealing from yourself. The law of cause and effect never sleeps. Do not get into the habit of accepting job offers from the dark side. They will always sell you a reason for vengeance. Where do you think the need to get even with someone comes from? Could it be to satisfy your ego? What feeds your ego? Your ego is the biggest supporter of your identity. It becomes hungrier with each unanswered prayer. However, the prayers get answered in time. You cannot give up.

Before you take the first step on the road to vengeance, think again. Because, if you come back from that trip, all you will have is a medal made of ice. And that medal will melt by the burning fire of regret that eventually visits you, back in this lifetime.

Think again. Channel that energy into forgiveness. **Release yourself from the cycles of chasing selfish, empty victories**. If you still want a medal, let a hungry person you feed draw you one in the silence of his heart. The good you do will never be unnoticed in this life.

Imagine putting all the fruits of vengeance in a juice maker and drinking it. How do you think it will taste? Sweet? You are wrong.

The initial sweetness of that poison is artificial, even if you are willing to drink it. Once it is in your bloodstream, it will alter your own chemicals and turn your immune system against you. Not only will it taste really bitter, but it will also stain your heart. Even if you cover up and hide it from everyone else, that stain may never come off your heart.

What is the antidote for such a poison that goes straight to the heart?

Try forgiveness, to begin with, and do not pretend as if you have already done your part. First of all, forgiveness should start with you. If you have made a mistake and believe it was the fault of others, you burn with your need for vengeance because your life has been turned upside down. But what do you think you will gain from such reasoning? Just remember that destroyed hopes and dreams are buried in the cemetery of wasted lives, including yours. Then what? When regret comes to haunt you, even during daylight, how far will you go to escape, if you can?

Regret does not recognize walls or locked doors. It grows bigger as your memories of mistakes start to visit you without an invitation. You cannot hide behind your stupidity. Your anger will not bail you out. The victim within you cannot keep your head high.

Accepting your mistake will cultivate the ground for seeds of regret. **Do not rush the cycles of nature.** Your grief will grow even in the hidden corners of your heart.

Forgiveness is not a step to achieve through any short cut. It will not work.You need to do your homework. While you are doing your homework, you will end up watching the same movie again and again. You will watch yourself making your mistake, forced to keep track of its ripples. It will not be easy. It may even feel like salt is dancing in your open wound, bullying you and testing you.

After you accept your mistake, do not assume you are done. Acceptance is just a start. How about taking responsibility? You will see that the basis of your action was conditioned by another happening. The action you took that resulted in your mistake could not have been carried out by a mindful person. Then what is the triggering factor that opened your subconscious mind and controlled you to commit such mistakes? Where is the internal warning device that can actually stop us before we make another mistake?

Perhaps the warning device is subject to being hacked. But by whom?

Could this be the reason for our own immune system to attack itself? Are we the ones actually destroying ourselves? If we realize this, how can we change it? Can we tell our cells not to attack themselves anymore? Can we bring peace into ourselves? Have no more internal wars? Is that possible?

Vanadium is an element used to harden steel. What element sets the sadness of *your* heart and causes it to seek vengeance? Can that element be used to make your compassion stronger? Can we become anything we want, if we just decode our own structure?

When we find ourselves in a mental or emotional state of being, is it by our choice? Or are we only reading lines from our life's script that was written for us? If we can choose what to *be*, why can't we choose what to *think* and how to *feel*?

Sabotaging ourselves is like punishing ourselves, because we dysfunctionally believe we don't deserve the reward. Maybe we were exposed to that belief while flowing in the current of the river of the oblivion. Perhaps it was just a billboard that got our attention, the way we are exposed to so many billboards with advertisement as we drive down the highway. We cannot read all of them, but some do stand out somehow. Why is that? Who are we listening to? What are we choosing to see? Why are we listening to the messages from the darkness, knowing they can be tricky?

Maybe the darkness told the light, while they were editing the screenplay of life, "How about, whenever a human being's desire arises, I should interfere?" Can the Vanadium of our being harden our faith in ourselves so the dark can never use desire against us? Can temptation be directed to create goodness in this life?

Suffering is a human being's Vanadium. It has a purpose. When it enters your life, you cannot ignore it. It will kick your pride, it will shatter your ego, it will beat you up, and it will shake your existence. Suffering will make you think about your regret and vengeance concurrently. Which one will you choose?

Regret will take you to the light, whereas vengeance will usher you toward the darkness.

Do not seek vengeance. If you plant its seeds in your heart, you will only reap darkness. It will keep you away from awakening. It will bury you in your own garden. Do not go after vengeance.

Let the regret teach you about humility. Let your humility show you you are a human being. In this life, there are mountains we can climb, but the same mountains also have cliffs from which we can fall.

Before you reach to the valley of forgiveness, you need to travel through the catacombs of your regret, swim in the depths of your despair, burn in the fires of your anger, build the bridges of your compassion, feed the light with your life, and share it with your kindness. When you travel, do not turn off your senses. Learn to forgive at your own pace. Learn to rise above with your own wings. Learn to let it go unconditionally. Forgiveness is like taking the dagger out of your heart and using it to cut off the shackles that keep you in the prison of life. Set yourself free.

Start your journey now. Do not wait! **The right time is *now*.**

19

VENOM OF ANIMUS

THE VENOM OF ANY malevolent ill will only flows back to its originator. The hatred you carry only defeats you, not anyone else. And compassion is your antidote.

When hatred starts to invade your thoughts, it can feel like your veins start to duplicate in no time. This invasion spreads throughout your body like an uninvited disease and takes over your mind, too. You might even forget why you are clinging to hatred and carry it like a torch. But you don't realize you have already set yourself on fire with that torch. You are too proud to see that you are on fire.

Hatred attacks your internal organs, but you may choose to ignore it because you think it is a game you'll surely win. But who really is the winner, when you play against yourself? The trap you masterfully build to capture your victim works brilliantly—by capturing you in the end. It is not something you can hide, either.

What would it take for you to see that the victim of your hatred is *you* and no one else? Why would you cut your heart out to feed the hatred?

The venom of your hatred will poison you, and your common

sense will suffer. It will keep you isolated, and you will only be invited to join fraudulent meditation practices hosted by hungry wolves. You will only be served crocodile tears to drink. So, are you game?

Turn yourself toward compassion. Let compassion cleanse the venom out of your system. Do not rush! Do not give up! Compassion will take you to the places and people you need. Your love calibrates higher than hatred. Remember the frequency. When you focus on hate, you operate at a level where you will start to fall further away from wisdom. You will not see clearly why hatred invaded your system in the first place. You will not understand the consequences that will spin off from your blind reasoning. You will hold onto your hate for… what? Finding peace?

Peace is not born out of ignorance. How are you going to transform hatred into compassion? Again, you do this one step at a time. First, start with something little. Literally. Like start feeding the fish in a bowl or mowing the lawn or watering the house plants. When you catch yourself being restless, take a deep breath. Volunteer your time to help others. Start with something small.

Then, move on to the person or thing that triggers you. Let's say that what triggers you is a person. Think a bit further, and remember the incident when your negative thoughts about that individual were created for the first time. Yes, this is your homework. You need to be committed. Even if that person said this or that about you or did this or that to you, can any of it be reversed? Can any of it be released? You cannot reverse it, but you can release it.

Do you know what you are releasing?

You are freeing yourself from the debris created by the animus's earthquakes. Otherwise, you will be crushed and buried under them. Yes, you do have a choice.

When you cling to it, you are actually attaching yourself to it.

When you are attached, you get hooked.

When you are hooked, you are no longer conscious.

When you are not conscious, you are not aware.

When you are not aware, you are sleepwalking.

When you are sleepwalking, you are walking in a park designed by the darkness.

The darkness is a place where you will continue to fall until there is no place left to go but down. If you want to rise above, you need to put the wings of compassion on your back. Just like any other fallen angel and light-worker, look up and believe you can rise.

Be thankful for the walks you have taken in the park of the darkness. Because, if it weren't for the darkness, you might have continued to take the light for granted. Be thankful for your suffering.

So, let go of your need to carry hatred on your shoulders. You will soon realize how heavy it is. Having a need for vengeance is not worth it. Let it go so you can set yourself free from it. Knock on the door of compassion and introduce yourself. Tell it you are new at this, but you are willing. **Nobody will be turned away from the house of compassion**. With so much suffering around us, there is a great need for the deliverers of compassion. Choose compassion over animus.

Venomous thoughts thrive in the minds of those who are not aware. When they release their poisonous arrow, they don't realize they can be hit by the same arrow, too. Such thoughts are brilliant manipulators. They can trick you quickly into buying a victory, but you end up coming home with a lifetime of misery, instead.

Even small consideration of such a poisonous action is enough to activate a chain of irreversible events. This fire of heedlessness can grow rapidly, like a forest fire, and consume you, as well. If you think your thoughts never travel through your body, you are incorrect. Not only does a thought travel, but it can move into an organ, where it starts nurturing a disease that has yet to arrive. Your thoughts and actions are important. They have the ability to form anything.

When you visualize the journey of thoughts, make sure it does not end at just "*thinking*." That is the beginning. It is like igniting a match on friction but then witnessing it turn into the fire that can burn anything in its path. It is one thing when it is a thought, but it can become a monster, if you choose to act on it. And if you spend enough time cultivating that venomous view, it will steal enough energy from your absent mind to get itself manifested. Like a ghost, your thought will channel itself into becoming an imprint on your energy. You may not be able to capture a ghost, but perhaps you can retrieve that thought of yours, provided it was yours to begin with.

Before you declare ownership of any thought that seems to beg your attention by screaming in your mind, take a deep breath. How much do you really want to invest in that thought? Perhaps you should "*think*" about that. Because thoughts are like dust particles in the air: they can go anywhere they want. The same dust particle can visit you while you sleep and also visit someone else who is breathing the same air somewhere else.

Beings on this planet are connected. Thoughts and feelings travel along unseen bridges between humans' energies. We may not comprehend why some thoughts and feelings just show up, but we still do not have to own them.

Just remember that the energy you put into any thought and feeling will make it grow bigger. So, do you really want to create a monster of animosity? Because, if you do, never assume you can tame it, thinking the monster will obey its originator. It will consume you, instead, and will achieve that through the energy of your regret.

Every human, regardless how stupid their mistakes, has the privilege of learning from them. Humans are all entitled to a chance to redeem themselves. Unfortunately, in some places on this planet, some people will not have this opportunity for redemption except by working on themselves. **No force can stop any human being from investing in themselves**.

It is never too late to get to know yourself. You can choose which thought your energy should feed on. Choose a healing one instead of a damaging one.

20

THRIVING IN SAVAGE PORTALS

WHEN YOU FIND YOURSELF lingering above, as if something took your spirit and left your physical body below, you better find something to hold onto, if you want to remain connected to your life.

Lost in strange harbors, waiting for ships to come and deliver you back to yourself, while hoping the dark clouds will surrender to blue skies—this may not be an easy journey for any of us. It is like finding your way back home in an unfamiliar forest: you never know if a monster or a fairy is waiting for you behind the trees. Not seeing it clearly in your mind's eye can also blind your sight and mute the rest of your senses. This is the perfect time for fear to come and lead you behind the trees, where the monster of your choice will be waiting for you. While you don't want to go there, you may believe you have no other option, because the ground you stand on turns steeply downhill. You cannot stop falling. You cannot stop thinking about the things that will cause anxiety. All you think about is the monster.

Actually, you have already met the monster. That monster of yours has already put you in this situation. However, you did not see that monster because your eyes were closed, your heart was not open, your mind was cloudy, and you were sleepwalking.

Welcome to the savage portals where your life awaits for your response and you feel paralyzed. How do you wake up from a coma?

It is entirely possible to awaken, if there is a communication between you and the world outside. You will be visited by both the darkness and the light when you are in a coma. It is like finding yourself in the river of oblivion and not being sure where the flow might take you. You will be exposed to any visitors who also have access to such portals. While your family and friends think you are dying, in fact you are just being offered the chance to experience different life scenarios.

In the case of your coma, you are in a depression due to your suffering. You well know you have the option to stay there and never come back. If you want to remain in depression, that portal will issue you a residency. The language spoken in such a place will not be understood by your family and friends. Your portal's music can only be heard at a particular frequency. Maybe the wolves will hear it, but most humans will not.

In your depression, your loneliness will be your company, along with those who have access to your portal. The letters you send from your portal will be sucked into a black hole on their way to your home. You will not understand why no one visits you anymore.

However, your depression is not permanent. You have been given a great opportunity to wake up. Yes, your garden may feel savage and you may think all you have are thorns but no roses. You may even start to believe it is about over for you.

Life can be over in a blink of an eye. Everything you wished you could do but did not do can disappear just like that. You can walk away from your life anytime you want. Before you do that, however, you should at least know that nothing is permanent and everything changes. Your depression is a by-product of suffering. When you feel like your energy is drained, you may decide not to start a journey to see all the wonders of the world. But there are still many things that you can do, so long as you don't give up.

There is a difference between *"giving up"* and *"surrendering."* When you give up on your life because you can no longer handle your suffering, you start to lose your faith in yourself and everything in your reality. When you surrender, you accept your suffering and no longer want to waste your energy working against the current of your soul's journey. When you surrender (not in religious terms), you know where you are. Your knowledge of having a human experience has carried you so far. You are now open to receive more knowledge. You just don't know where to get it. All you need is another dose of hope downloaded into you. Yes, it is free.

The next time you think you have lost hope because your garden has turned savage, do not stop watering the ground. You may not see the fruit of your watering right away, as the water needs to reach the roots first. Just like you need to visit your early life in order to get some answers, and just like you need to go to the roots of your suffering, the trees in your garden need to receive the water of life through their roots. Then, life will be carried up to its branches, just like hope will once again find its way to your heart. When the tree blossoms, you will blossom as well with the light of hope in your eyes.

Figure out why you stopped watering your garden in first place. But remember, blaming anyone, including yourself, will not take you to the oasis where you can access water. It is more important to accept what is happening as it is. Do not try to figure out who did what and why. Just notice and accept the fact that your garden needs help.

Get up! Take a shower, if you can. Wake up!

Remember, if you fall into a dark place in your life, shouldn't it be possible to think about light places, as well? If your trees gave you fruit before, isn't it possible to at least imagine that can happen again?

Your next move starts with imagining and visualizing first. Why not visualize a path of your own that will take you to the end of your suffering? Are you willing to see?

21

EQUANIMITY IN HYSTERIA

HOW DO YOU stay calm when it feels like the ground you stand on just swallowed you up? How do you stay focused when it feels like the air you breathe is filled with poison? How do you stay alive when it feels like your heart has been broken into pieces?

Humans are amazing beings. They can handle more pressure than volcanos can. They can stand still against tornadoes that would topple sequoias. They can fly higher than eagles.

Humans are gentle beings. They melt in sufferings when butterflies would not. They fall apart at their disappointments when little toys would not. They lose their faith at their first failure where an autumn leaf would not.

Human beings are part steel and part cotton candy. They have wings on their backs and iron anchors on their feet. They have enough hope to reach the sky but also fears great enough to pull them underground.

In their perfect imperfection, they can be anything they want to be. A mother can defeat a lion to save her child. A father can travel to the end of the rainbow to bring gold for his daughter. But a simple word can be big enough to cut off their life supply. A mere disappointment can destroy their flowers. Simple loneliness is never simple for them.

Life between hot and cold, the north of joy and the south of sadness, the west of hope and the east of relinquishing, above disappointments and under guilt, can mold human beings into unpredictable shapes. Humans can walk to the end of the universe but can also simply give up and remain stoic.

Healing, however, does not happen alone. There is always something or someone, seen or unseen, that plays a role in life's healing process.

So, when it feels like the ground has swallowed you, when you can no longer breathe the poisonous air or when your heart has been broken into pieces, do not fight! When all you have is the blanket of hysteria in the eye of a winter storm, you have to continue repeating back to yourself that the storm is not permanent.

Of course, you are likely saying, "Sure... Yeah... Yup..." It is not so easy to believe that the storm will come to an end. The difference between the ones who turn their hysteria into equanimity and those who do not is the will to survive and end their suffering. They start to pay attention to those who have fallen before them. They start to listen to those who have visited the darkness. They start to realize that many of us suffer in our own ways. Then they make a commitment to learn from their experience in hysteria. They start practicing equanimity. No matter how little the steps they take, they know, with every passing day, they continue to get closer to ceasing the suffering.

Equanimity is available to all of us. It starts with accepting your situation. But, again, do not judge: neither the situation nor yourself.

This will take time. It will be more difficult in the beginning. At first, you will notice more of what is negative than is positive in your life. You will complain about the negative aspects of your life because you have so many of them. You will yearn for the positive side of life, because you miss it so much. A solution to your struggle lies in the middle. You will feel lighter when you release the weight of carrying both the negative and the positive.

Calm can be achieved when you are no longer attached to the drama of your reality. Acquiring a state of mind where you figure out how not to cling or get hooked or attached may be easier for some, but maybe not for you. You cannot compare your hysteria to someone else's. For you to learn to calm yourself, you need to keep your mind in your body. You can do this by focusing on your breath.

Simple?

Your breath reminds you that you are alive. That is good, isn't it? Your mind, on the other hand, will take you on a trip to the end of the universe. On the way back from your journey, you will be visited by every single forgotten and unwanted memory from your past. Amazing, right? So, how do we keep the mind in the body?

You will be required to stay calm, so your mind cannot pull you in each and every direction. **Meditation is a fantastic way to practice equanimity.** Let's say you are trying to calm yourself down by taking a deep breath. The first thought that comes to your mind could be something like, *Why did I do that?*

Now stop. Here are some possible avenues to consider:

A: Okay. This is just a thought. I hear it, but I will now take a deep breath instead.

OR

B: What? Where did that come from? What did I do? I wonder if my subconscious mind is trying to tell me something. Is this about the little white lie I told the other day? I cannot believe I thought of that. Why did I remember that? I still don't know what I did. Could this be about the future? Oh no! Am I going to do something stupid? Wow! My nose is really itchy. Oh no! My stomach is growling. I wonder what everyone will think..." Blah, blah, blah...

You see how easy it is to be sucked into downward-spiraling thoughts? Each thought can create many new ones, if you cling to it. If you do not want weeds in your flower garden, stop watering the weeds.

So, does option A seem any better to you?

When a thought arises in your mind while you are practicing equanimity, do not give any energy to that thought. You will be sucked into creating more of it. This applies whether it is a positive or a negative one.

We are creative beings. Our imagination should not be contained. So, the mind itself is the king of its own land. The mind can be flirtatious, tricky, demanding, controlling, imaginative, magical, and more. Let me emphasize the word "*tricky.*" It will play games with you, and you may not even be aware of which team you are on.

So, when a thought comes to you, simply say, "Okay, this is just a thought." And then let it go.

Letting go will require practice. Do it and practice it every time you can. Never label it by saying, "Hmmm... Interesting...," because you will get hooked right away. Once you are hooked, the rest will follow, and you will be trapped. Before you know it, you will be wondering if your great-great-great-grandmother's second distant cousin's nephew had anything to do with the sightings of vampires.

Let it go. The more you are attached, the faster your mind will create scenarios for you. And you will not be able to stop it, unless you start practicing equanimity. Because only then will you change the frequency of your thought process.

22

HEEDLESS JOURNEY

A HEEDLESS JOURNEY is like going to the moon for the first time and choosing to stay in your spaceship and play video games, instead of stepping outside to soak up all the experiences of being on the moon.

Many of us go through life without understanding what life is actually all about. We skip through events as if they were only meant to be remembered by the pictures we take. We have beautiful memories, but sometimes they get lost in the chaos of our sad memories. Unfortunately, **sometimes, the people who will help us to become wiser are delivered to us in a box of challenges and turmoil**. When we go through that chaos, we put the experience on a piece of paper and stick it between the pages of a book titled, *Heedless Journey,* so we will never again remember it.

However, we miss a great opportunity when we fail to learn from our experiences. We waste those learning opportunities, if we never open and read the book written by the wise.This is not an easy journey to undertake. Most of us barely survive its chaos, not to mention we never want to remember it afterwards. When we struggle, we should see it as an opportunity to learn from the experience.

We may fall by ourselves, but when we get up, we can help lift up many others who have fallen, too. The well we have fallen into will invite many other humans to fall into it, as well. But if you tell those who cannot seem to find their way out how you climbed all the way up by stepping on the steps of your own humility, perhaps your wisdom can save them, too.

Anything you experience is recorded in the book of your life. When your physical life is over, your book of life is shared in a classroom where the elders teach the younger generations. Some of those who are there will be interested in your journey. The things you have missed and taken for granted; the mistakes you have made and the upset you have caused; as well as the smiles you have put on people's faces, and the hand you gave to those whenever they needed one. Through this, the newcomers will learn the planet Earth is a very special place where its occupants are exposed to opposites all the time, which is how they build memories and learn.

In your book of life, the pages are never torn out. For each day of life, a page is reserved. Some pages will have many stories to tell, while some may have nothing on them. **Do not let your human experience be nothing.** Make sure there is something on each page of your life. You are part of the flow of universal energy. Do not assume that your emptiness will not affect the rest of us.

Be mindful. Do not miss this amazing gift called life. Do not let heedlessness be the scribe of your memoir.

Be thankful. Not every human being is aware of their journey.

Life is shared. You carry your portion of it. So, when your loved one is down, you are down, too. Some burdens are visible, and some are not.

Because you don't see what it is hidden behind someone's sorrow, do not assume that a person is not damaged. Remember, we all can get lost, and some of us may never find their way back. Sometimes, all a lost person needs is light. Do not let someone fight alone, with sharks circling him in the ocean of his sorrow. Let your helping hand and compassionate heart become the lighthouse on his safe shores. Help him find his way.

If you only travel for selfish reasons, can you still find someone who is truly interested in your journey? What will you tell them, when you show them your pictures taken by a stranger with your big head glowing in front of the city skyline? Do you think you can cover up your insincerity? Do you think people won't figure you out? If you come across the fountain of healing, won't you be sharing it with all living beings?

Whatever you do or do not do, you create new stories to be written in your book of life. Your story can inspire someone else. The picture you took can create hope in someone's heart. Try to see that this life is for everyone and the world we share is the reflection of who we are. Why would we destroy this place? Then again, if someone is not interested in his own healing, would he even care about others', let alone the world's healing?

Constant selfishness **is a heedless journey**. There will be times when some of your actions could really be categorized as selfish. Here, we are not talking about going to a movie theater by yourself as an act of being selfish. Instead, we are talking about only feeding yourself and not your children, when there is not enough food for everyone.

Ignorance **is a heedless journey**. Not being interested in anything other than yourself will only lock you inside the castle of your vanity. That is the place where you cannot live happily ever after and where your only companion will be the silent mirror.

Greed **is a heedless journey**. You may not realize it, but when you compete to consume more than you need, your eyes will never be satisfied and your heart will remain empty. You will not find anything to fill the emptiness, unless you sign a contract, which is a lifetime curse, of course, because, with that contract, everything you touch will turn to gold. And yet, with all that gold in your life, your heart will never be warm.

Envy **is a heedless journey**. It will age you before your time. First, your heart will go on a strike. When there is no blood available to water your tree of life, your branches will dry on your forehead. The lines around your eyes will not be caused by laughter, but by the spite in your eyes.

Fakeness **is a heedless journey**. Wasting your life by living in fictitious stories you write may garner you an award so dense, it can suffocate you in the middle of your acceptance speech. Get real and get to know yourself.

Anyone who is not awake is travelling on the road of remiss. During their travel, they will be exposed to some beautiful sunrises and sunset, but will they notice? There will be tornadoes and earthquakes, but will they see?

When you see only what you want to see, are you not limiting your senses?

If you are not mindful, then what could possibly be going through your head? Unless you have reached a mental state where no more attachment is happening to any of your thoughts, there has to be something else, another thought to occupy you. Is that not a choice then? If you are more concerned with one thing but not another, are you not choosing where to put your energy? Do you think being absentminded does not require any of your energy?

Sometimes, you may not get a second chance to repeat what you have missed. When you use your senses, you use energy. When it comes to being mindful, it is about being able to quiet down the mental chattering so you can turn the volume down. When you are alone, practice being mindful. When you are around others, practice listening. Mindfulness can be learned by practicing. It is not a competition. It is not only for certain people. **The journey you are on is only possible through others' contributions.**

Not everyone creates their own hole and then falls in it. However, when we fall, were we really being careful? Don't you want to understand why your steps took you near that hole?

What do we listen to when our minds are dancing with many thoughts? Which one do you choose? How do you choose? And based on your desire or your need?

Perhaps mindfulness is leaving the channels open for information to arrive, but you still get to decide what information enters and definitely what information leaves. Because, sometimes, when we think we have processed a thought, the words we choose to express it may not be the right ones.

We need to care, and we need to pay attention. Being mindful requires that we care. Do not be careless. Remain connected to yourself while still caring for others. Do not get lost in the past or the future, because it always is about *now*. When you start to drift away in your thoughts, bring yourself back to the moment you are in. Whatever happens receives its fuel from the current moment. If you have no energy to save your *now*, what are you going to do?

23

VANISHING VANITY

ONCE UPON A TIME, there was a man who had the most scintillating, magical mirror hanging on the walls of his vainglorious existence. Anything he wanted to hear, the magical mirror would tell him. He was incomparable to anything and unmatched, except for his own reflection in the magic mirror, which he had created out of his immortal vanity.

This man was above anything when he flew. From his vantage, he only saw a little, and it was enough for him. He already knew everything.

One day, he noticed a tiny crack in the mirror. He got overwhelmed with such a repellant imperfection. He tried to cover it, but every time he looked at his reflection, the crack waited for him patiently.

It took his ego a long time to realize that the crack was indeed nothing but a cut on his forehead he was never willing to look at. His disappointment grew faster than his pride that day. He did not understand who could ever dare damage such beauty.

Even his magic mirror could not answer him, as the mirror was only as wise as he. The man chose not to see his cut. Soon after, his ego was triggered unexpectedly. He noticed that the growing scar was becoming a deciduous tree, extending from his forehead down to the rest of his body. He looked at his reflection in the mirror fearfully. The mirror could not tell him that his ego was becoming a leafless tree. For the first time, the man felt something very unfamiliar. A tiny teardrop fell down his cheek and touched his heart. This was a strange happening for him. He stood there motionless. As his branches grew bigger, his mirror of vanity started to disappear.

Once, he used to fly above everything. Now, this man who became a tree felt shackled deep into the ground by his roots. He yearned for freedom. He wanted his wings back, and he wanted to hear his mirror, but his wishes were not answered.

One day, the bird of synchronicity landed on one of this man's branches. The bird could see the man within the tree. The man yelled from the roots of his existence and asked the bird, "Do you know who did this to me?"

The bird said, "I used to look for the same answer myself, a long time ago. Nobody could tell me what had happened to my beautifully colored feathers. I was the most beautiful bird in the forest. Admittedly, I thought it had to be because of other birds' envy."

"Did you then find who did that to you? Since you now have your beautiful feathers back?"

"Yes, but I cannot tell you how. You need to find it out yourself. But I can say one thing. The answer you are looking for is not far from the tree."

The tree felt hollow when the bird flew away.

Seasons passed and touched the tree's leafless branches, but the man still had no answer. He started to feel something inside one day for the first time. This feeling could not be ignored or stopped. It traveled all over his body and shook every branch of the tree.

He found himself lost and felt overwhelmed by the responses of his body. His tears turned into rivers and ran through his entire body. Everywhere the water touched, a leaf started to grow. Each leaf transformed into a cradle and started to rock the seedlings of fruit. The tree did not question as he surrendered to the magic of what was happening to him. Then the seeds turned into fresh fruit. One day, the first ripe fruit fell on the ground. The tree remembered what the bird had told him: that the answer he was looking for was not far from the tree.

As he kneeled down for the first time in his life, the tree lowered his branches all the way to the ground to pick up his fruit. As he picked it up off the ground, he could not believe what he saw: a universe under his feet that he had never noticed. There were all kinds of beings right next to his roots. He realized that while all he had wanted to see was above, he had never imagined all this life was down by his feet.

He held the fruit in his hand and said, "You are my first offspring. Even though you look tiny, I know you have more wisdom than any magic mirror can reveal. Your name must be humility, as I now remember what a little bird once told me."

Human life can take an unexpected turn. It can snow in the middle of your summer. You can lose your voice right before your crescendo. What are you going to do when that happens? Maybe it will not happen to you, right?

Vanity is hollow. It is like a bottomless pit. And like a stomach with no limits, your hunger for it will never be fully satisfied. You'll consume empty calories, hoping to build some muscle, but will only reserve you a seat at the nosebleed level of comprehension. Vanity is a drug of choice, and it is addictive. It will alter your chemistry and come with many side effects.

Sooner or later, your body will have to face those side effects. But nothing will seize your addiction to vanity the way humility will. **Humility is the antidote for vanity**.

Is your need for vanity embedded in your deoxyribonucleic acid? Is ego an essential constituent of your chromosomes? Is it an unconditionally given gift of heredity? Or did your environment give that to you?

Even if you were born with it, is it worth it to feed such an invasive and controlling monster? Because the more you practice, the faster your identity will be built on a fault line, and the inevitable earthquake will cause your ego to fall into pieces. Unless you do your research before building your home on any piece of land, you will purchase the shell of your identity in the state of sleepwalking. And someday, if you luckily wake up, you will realize that your identity, protected by your vanity, has taken a great deal of your energy.

Channel vanity into modesty. When you do a favor, no one needs to know. You do not need to put your good deeds on your résumé.

How do you measure your worth? What do you think your worth is? It is subjective, isn't it? Can you put a price on your life, or any other being's life, for that matter? Where does the entitlement to vanity come from? If vanity is the ground of your garden, then humility will not grow there. If you take off with vanity, you may crash land with humility.

There has always been some rivalry going on somewhere in this world. It is almost impossible to ignore. Someone comes up with an idea, and someone else tries to trash it; someone defends this, and someone attacks it. **Perhaps all that tension between opposites is there for us to learn from**. Maybe it is an opportunity to exercise mindfulness. But do you have to take a side?

If vanity and humility are rivals, what is the middle way? Perhaps too much of anything can tip the balance. Otherwise, how can someone understand the impact of humility, if not for their pride? Then again, there are many people who never even get close to either vanity *or* humility. Are their harsh lessons only for those who live on the edge?

When you think of equanimity, imagine a place like home, very peaceful. Imagine your heart is your home, and this home of yours is built between the highest mountains and overlooks the deepest ocean. Something in you keeps telling you that you should always be at the very top of that mountain. Meanwhile, someone else has a house like yours, built in a very similar location, and that person has no need or interest in being on top of the mountain.

If the top of the mountain represents vanity, if you fall, you will hit the bottom of the deepest ocean, which is humility.

However, not everyone's learning experience will be that

dramatic, because it doesn't have to be. When you fall from so high, you may be given a great opportunity to learn from your failure.

Now, why would you want to set up such a harsh learning experience, in the first place? Do you wonder? Do you think the roses atop that mountain smell better than those in your own garden? Is it our curiosity that makes us different than the rest of the world? Do we yearn to be different? Why is that?

Where does the desire "to be someone" come from? Why do we have to become someone? Do we fail so we can learn more about ourselves? If that is the case, are we truly failing? Or are we creating an opportunity to recognize ourselves?

24

TRIGGERING HUFFY

IT'S NOT REALLY that difficult to trigger anyone who is already annoyed or irritated.

Anyone who is displeased in general is unaware that the shell they live in is in complete disarray and has many tentacles that operate independently. They are too quickly triggered every time their tentacles get close to anything and blame the ocean, because it was in their way. They blame the centuries-old trees, because they just showed up on their path out of nowhere. They blame the sun for being too bright and believe there are simply too many stars at night. It is as if they are programmed to be triggered.

Are you a huffy? If you are, your tentacles can be controlled and even eliminated, since they only exist within your imagination.

A huffy's aura invades your personal space, but he will think *you* are in *his* space. He will bully you, because you are part of his universe. And he will create a scenario to be triggered by someone or something. Try to imagine having a life like theirs, where nothing is right, nothing is acceptable, and nothing is good. What message do they send? And who is receiving their messages?

Being triggered is like being hooked. It is a form of suffering.

When you get triggered, your frequency shifts and you lose your ability to remain calm. And what do you think happens when you are inhaling fire and exhaling fire? You will definitely burn yourself, along with those closest to you. And if you think your anger, frustration, irritation, resentment, moodiness, and crankiness will not burn anything or anyone, you are a fool. And the game the fool plays is destined to be lost.

Is there anything out there that can put out your fire? Do you have to play this game? If you do, what do you think you will win? How can you win, when you defeat the ones you love the most? How can you enjoy that victory when it is built upon the shoulders of the weak? How can you reverse their disappointment in you? How can you continue to believe that your truth is the ultimate one?

In this life, we are exposed to the negative, so you need to recognize the positive. We are exposed to anger, so you need to believe in peace. We are introduced to hatred so that you will surrender to love.

Do you really want to be so ignorant as to miss all the trains in your life? Do you really want to miss out on opportunities to be with anyone you want, anywhere you want? Once again, wake up!

Just remember: some trains are traveling only one way. Sometimes, it may not be easy to put back together a broken heart. Bear in mind that identity is an experience. You do not have to be whatever it is that is making you unhappy. Think again whether or not being a huffy is actually working out well for you. Is it?

Can crankiness be cured? Do we inherit it? Or does it pass on to us from the environment in which we live?

We are exposed to a great deal of unfairness in life. When the frequency of external grumpiness takes up residence in our internal headquarters, we are once again presented with an opportunity to chose whether we want to be attached to it or not.

The energy of hypersensitivity, anger, irritation, resentment, quarrelsomeness, and many of their close relatives calibrate at a level where mindfulness will not visit. When you reside in their neighborhood, you will live with the consequences of being part of that type of energy. Such neighborhoods are really not into social gatherings and definitely not into receiving solicitors. They simply do not want you.

And there are people like that. No matter what is happening, they are usually irate and ill-humored. Their skin is like an invisible fence: if you get too close, it will zap you. Why do you think that is? Doesn't being irritable take a lot of energy? What are we gaining by simply being against anything or anyone? Do we have to broadcast our disagreements? Why can't we let our thoughts rest a little, before they turn into unwise words and escape from our paralyzed mouths?

Could it be, perhaps, that we use our grumpiness to let those who are around us know what we are unhappy about so, hopefully, the universe will give us what we want? Focusing on what you *don't* want and making sure everyone knows what you don't like, clarifying what frustrates you and pushing people away are going to distract you from being lighter. **Your awakening may not find its way through the obstacles you create in your own labyrinth**. You may not realize that focusing on such intense negativity will only use its own seeds to bring more of it.

The universe has a dry sense of humor sometimes. It lets your pet peeves follow you around. The farther away you want to be from what annoys you, the closer the universe brings those things or people to you. Why is that? Is it really the universal law? Are we attracting it? Well, are we not magnetic? If we can bring more of what we don't want, shouldn't we be able to bring more of what we *do* want?

All it really takes to tame annoyance is learning tolerance. Yes, this requires practice, too. Tolerance starts with respect, which eventually trains you to become nonjudgmental, so long as you stick with it. When you show respect, when you no longer judge, and when you share your light, you will no longer need to think about pushing yourself to be tolerant.

Tolerance may not come naturally. We may feel like we are pushing the boundaries of something, but that "something" is nothing other than your identity. If your identity is against so many things, does that mean you are controlled by your identity?

25

VIRTUOUS VENTURES

WHEN YOU MAKE A decision to choose, what do you think your decision is based upon?

Do you get up and say, "Today is a great day to make someone's life hell"? Do you say, "You know, I think I am going to destroy my neighbor's vegetable garden today"?

There are people out there who are not mindful of what they say or do. Some people are hypnotized by the idea of accumulating financial wealth alone; they don't care how they earn money or what their livelihood is.

But, just like everything else, your livelihood is a representation of your life's frequency. Sooner or later, it will calibrate itself to match your earnings to your original investment. If you are producing fake medicine for the sick and selling it on the black market, you are signing a contract with your blood without knowing whom it's with.

Your frequency will take you to your match in life. When you think you are winning, in fact, you might be burying yourself. The energy that keeps your false venture going will eventually run out of its supply, if you do not change its foundation. You cannot fool everyone all the time. You will know if you are doing the right thing to earn income and make a living. **Your choice of livelihood can take you to the darkness or the light.**

Imagine how everything is connected. The fake medicine you sell will find its buyer. But what you may not realize is that the one who buys it is also in a circle of his own right or wrong livelihood. There is always an energetic exchange. The bad energy you offer travels around the universe to come back and find you. In the end, you may end up buying what you sold in the first place. But it will be labeled differently. Whatever you give will come back.

Virtuosity should not be wasted. Your curious mind can offer you many avenues to explore. You may find the unfamiliar path more attractive. When it comes to making a choice about what you want to do with your life, your decision may not always be based on wisdom. Although we may pursue a particular career path, we can never be sure what other openings may be presented to us in that life.

Regardless where we might be—which cobblestone of life we are standing on, which trees we target to climb, or what waters we want to catch our fish from—there still is one thing we should pay close attention to. Be mindful.

Some people are terrific magicians. They seem to be able to pull anything you want out of their hats. You will be hypnotized by their charm, ecstatic at the prize you are given. We all participate in those shows. There is always a magician behind the choices we make. Sometimes, a part of us wants to escape from the ordinary. Some of us turn to something or someone stronger than us. Some turn to their magicians, and some worship the sun while others pray to the moon. There will be those who donate and those who steal; some who build and some who destroy; some will rise, and some will fall. Wherever you go, these opposites will be there. It will be up to you whether you choose a venture while sleepwalking or not.

Your existence in this life holds great power. You are capable of bringing absolute happiness or destruction. Do you think we have learned from all the wars and the disagreements that have taken place between humans and destroyed so many lives? Some of us will continue to do our work so there will be peace, but some of us will insist on engineering weapons to destroy it all.

We make decisions based on many things, but if greed, pride, ego, vengeance, hostility, and delusion are controlling the process, unfortunately the outcome will not be pretty.

Immortality is not a virtue. It is a soul-collector disguised as a promise-maker. Under its swan-like wings hide the desires of a vulture. You need to study its energy so you can recognize it the next time. You will be visited by it more than once. You cannot rely on your mind, because the promise-maker is already a *part* of your mind. You also need to listen to your body and your heart. **Before you dive into the lake of any venture, you need to find out how deep it is.**

Starting a new endeavor can be tempting. So you could very well be sleepwalking at the time of your decision. Like being taken by the songs of sirens, your own ignorance can bewitch your common sense, as you get ready to choose your venture.

26

BOOMERANG OF INTENTION

YOU MAY HAVE heard the saying, "What goes around comes around." Do you believe it?

Some people may not understand it, as they might only be satisfied by seeing an instant result. They think, if someone does something wrong, he should get his punishment right away. If he does something good, he should get his reward right away.

Well, the universal laws likely do not agree with you on your need for instant gratification. The time frame you are familiar with is just one of the definitions used in the dimensions of life. Just because you do not witness the result doesn't mean it hasn't happened or it won't occur.

Also, comprehending the true meaning of the timing of the effect created by your intention can be tricky, because the results may not be delivered in a way you expect or are accustomed to, but they will be delivered regardless of your being aware or not. The challenge here is setting your expectations, because your expectations will keep you lingering in the prison of life in which you are booked. Life can pass you by while you wait for your expectations be met, and you may miss many seasons of your life while you wait.

You have probably already figured out that life operates at the level of some unpredictability. Things can change any second. Someday, you may actually end up confessing to yourself that you know nothing at all, and that statement won't be incorrect. If you really think about it, what you *think* you know might be based on your knowledge of the past. You will be unaware of what is happening in the moment if you are not awake. And when you distracted, your mind steals your current moment and uses it in an unknown future.

Life is very enigmatic. We are all part of it in our own esoteric ways. We can be so sensitive, yet stoic. We are kaleidoscopic yet monochromatic at the same time. We receive punishment and reward through life. We can be benevolent under the armor of our own stern nature. We can be parsimonious with our time when it comes to helping others, but we don't mind spending money in the hopes we can buy love. We are never more than a second away from altering the life we've been gifted with.

Your boomerang may not only hit its target on its flight but, when you are not expecting, come back and hit you, too. Depending on your intention when you throw it, it will either turn into iron or feather. What would you prefer to be hit by? How do we know that our boomerang will hit its target?

If you throw your boomerang with a vengeance, it will come back and hit you with guilt. If you throw the guilt back, it will come back and hit you with shame. If you throw the shame back, it will hit you with loneliness. No matter how brilliantly you try to avoid it, the boomerang you throw will hit you back, either directly or indirectly.

Is it possible to be hit indirectly? For a moment, imagine yourself at the center of the universe. Go ahead! Don't be shy. Many of us already operate under that notion, as if it is our birthright anyway. Go ahead! Join the club.

Okay, now you are the center of the universe. Look around you. You might notice you are surrounded by many things and beings. Expand your vision a bit more. Become more global. Notice your connection to those who live in different countries. Great! Now imagine a light connecting you to all of those things and places. Perhaps you must be the center of the universe, after all.

Your boomerang and the light you have both operate at the same frequency. Your boomerang is assigned only to you. It will never function or even move in the hands of anyone else. It is designed so amazingly that it reads your DNA and becomes activated accordingly.

The boomerang is a part of you. This means it has access to all of your connections, regardless of their location. This access comes with unlimited freedom and willpower. So, your boomerang literally can hit anyone or anything in your circle. While you may celebrate your victory early, your boomerang, fueled with your stupidity, can travel all over the world and hit one of your connections, but you would not even hear about it. Because we are in this together, the boomerang cuts your friend's forehead, but you would end up with the scar on your soul. And if you do not look into your soul, you may never see your scars.

Some of us don't even realize when we've been hit by our own boomerang. We take our daily walks in Neverland, not knowing where we are. These hits get recorded in the book of your life. You can read it, if you want, but if you are a pompous being, you probably won't. Being a pompous person, of course, you would assume that you already have the privilege of having memorized every line written in that book, anyway.

One of the best things you can do for yourself and the universe is to slow down and read the book of your life, so you can reflect on it. Maybe then you will see the travel notes about your boomerang. Maybe then you will follow each step of its journey. Maybe then you will track down one particular recent hit that you have not been able to figure out.

You may have been wondering why, all of a sudden, you are no longer in a relationship or why you are no longer employed or many more endless questions. Go back to the book and start turning pages with thirst until you come across the exact page where it is revealed the day when you threw that boomerang at someone or something with that specific intention. Just like that!

Not every result, response, answer, solution, or reaction is instant. Some can take a lifetime, and some even can go beyond. That is because your boomerang might skip you, during your lifetime. But it doesn't mean you are off the hook, because it still can hit one of your connections. Hurt is also contagious. Learn to be compassionate.

Your intention has a tremendous effect on everything you do in life. It can provide you with joy, or it can allow you to experience wrath. The way you set your intention is also recorded in your book of life.

If you knew better about the law of the boomerang, would you still continue to be careless about the power of your intentions? If you knew it could not only damage you but also others, would you still go after your hollow need for revenge? When you throw your boomerang with anger, do you realize that you set it on fire? Have you noticed that, on its way back into your reality, it can burn your harvest? Would you throw it with ignorance, not caring about the value of life and not noticing how your boomerang hits yet another orphan child into the deepest hole of hunger? Would you throw your boomerang with selfishness and still live in your palace when you knew there are so many people trying to survive the nakedness of being homeless?

Is it okay to be removed from this life at such a level that you do not care about anything or anyone?

Your intention is like your collateral, but you do not have to take a loan out against it. You may not be able to pay it off. It is like spending what you don't have. Therefore, wrongly set intentions will be charged a very high interest rate that your lifetime may not be long enough pay it back. Do you want your family and friends to pay what you could not?

There is always a response in life. Some are visible, and some are not.

27

PAYING FOR YOUR STUPIDITY

THE RESULT OF ANY thoughtless action can, unfortunately, harm many people other than its owner. It can damage more than you, and some whom you hurt may never forgive you for it. You can spend a lifetime earning their forgiveness, or you can start investing in loving yourself again.

Always start your redemption process with yourself. Otherwise, you may find yourself asking for forgiveness from mermaids on the tops of the trees. Not everyone knows how to forgive. Although forgiveness can earn a human his or her wings, most of us still don't know how to forgive honestly and sincerely. Instead, we continue to be judgemental in our imperious, ignorant ways. Those of us who think we are superior to another being will find ourselves, sooner or later, burning in our own fire, feeling desperately cursed. We, too, need to redeem our own stupidity.

We all can make mistakes and take wrong turns. It does not seem like we arrived in this life with instructions, so, naturally, we walk between the fields of good deeds and mistakes. We can visit either place at any time. Some of us are too proud to confess our errors, and some of us are too stubborn to go back. Some of us are still asleep and the fields of mistakes become our bed. Some of us are so clueless, we don't even think we have made a mistake.

However, both fields are open to the public with no restrictions. Anyone can visit there at any time.

Redemption begins with small steps. Depending on the level of your stupidity and other people's perception of it, you may never be able to free yourself from your need to be forgiven by them. Do not waste your time. Those people may never be ready to let go of your stupidity, even after you have taken full responsibility for your mistake.

Redemption is initiated when you start to cleanse your heart, mind, body, soul, and place where you live. You are now your own goal and target. Your intention should be to understand and accept yourself. Once you acknowledge your mistake, start to think about how to move forward without avoiding or ignoring the facts that led to your slip and fall. Again, remember: this is not about blaming anyone or anything.

Do you think you can see the good within you? Do you think you can allow those who want to help to visit and offer you some advice during your time of confusion and loneliness? Do you think perhaps you are willing to learn from what you have done? Do you think you will be supported in your petition for redemption?

You *will* be supported in this journey, whether you are willing to acknowledge it or not. Here is a warning: Your support may not come from those whom you hope it will. Remember: do not expect! Do not set yourself up! When you release the ones who don't show up, you will have more space in your heart for new supporters to come in. Leave the door open. Do not be afraid.

If you are willing to see and accept, the support will be there for you. But you cannot allow yourself to become the victim of your own drama. Otherwise, your victim state of mind will lock the doors from inside, and no one else will be able to enter.

When you need help, get out of your own way. If you think asking for help is humiliating, you have a long way to go. Besides, humility is perfect for those of us who believed we could carry the globe between the horns of our stubborn heads of hay. When you need help, ask for it. Do not say you don't need it. You need help, and the universe has plenty of it to offer. Take it.

Your redemption will not be completed overnight. Your tears and heartache will most likely be kneaded into the dough of your suffering. You may even add your loneliness and being misunderstood into the batter. However, never forget to add your hope and faith, love, and wishes to become wiser, as well. Your dough will absorb the fire of the sun, the comfort of the wind, the cleansing magic of water, and the flour of the earth's harvest. You will notice you've had all of the ingredients you needed all along, but may have forgotten about them as you lost your way and became delusional.

Why do you think we lose our way anyway? How do you know the way you thought you lost was actually yours?

The roads to awakening are designed in exquisite harmony, so you will never be on just one road during your life. Most of the roads will feel safe, as you may not want to take chances by changing your journey. Sometimes knowingly and sometimes unknowingly, we change the lanes and find ourselves on unfamiliar roads. We may get panicky or become scared in strange territories. We may even think it could take a long time to become accustomed to our new path. But humans are resilient and can choose to resist the laws of disappointment. They can linger in their confusion and hopelessness for a while, but it can also stand up after taking a fall.

When you think your life has taken a wrong turn, maybe it actually did not. When you think you have failed, maybe you did not. When you think you have lost it all, maybe you have not.

Your fall could be your biggest opportunity to wake up. Your mistake could be one of the greatest blessings of your life. Your so called *"wrong turn"* could be the exact turn you needed to take. If you can learn to go with the flow sometimes, you will see that it consumes less of your energy. When you have more energy, you can start to plant flowers on the road to your new home. When you accept, you take the first step toward redeeming yourself. When you know you don't have to give up on your life, the wrong path you thought you landed on turns into a flying carpet and takes you to the land of freedom. Who knows? Maybe you will pick up a few more passengers on the way.

28

DEPRAVED PATHS

MAKING IMMORAL decisions can be easy to do but their consequences can be hard to digest. Perhaps you already are aware of some people who often make such decisions.

How do we fall into the belly of the world's washing machine, where we are spun again and again? Why do some of us keep repeating the same mistake over and over? Is that written in our destiny? Is there a magnetic field that keeps us bound to particular experiences so we cannot avoid them? Are we bound to certain people so we cannot get away from? Are we a chessman on a chess board and can only be moved by the hand that decides our destiny? If so, who are the other players?

When an opportunity presents itself to us, we need to understand that we are partly responsible for its arrival. You may not realize it at that moment, but you are a co-producer of your experience. At every opportunity, you can choose your response *only* if you are aware, in the moment. If you are not, you are about to trip.

Watch for signs around you when you choose a friend or a friend chooses you. If that person wants you to do something that is immoral, it means you are being presented with an opportunity to respond. And your response at that moment will define your future. If immorality is your choice, what do you think will happen after that? Your immoral decision will take you to a place where you will be asked whether you are interested in making other immoral decisions or not.

While you contemplate, keep in mind, literally speaking, that your first decision has already generated a cell within your body that will multiply the very moment you make your second immoral move. Basically, you are now the producer of your own show. Soon, you will become a tycoon, building your network of cells that are ready to be activated at a higher power, should you choose to make another depraved move. At that level, it might be a little late for you to turn back, because, by then, the craving for decadence will already have been activated. Just like a programmed robot, you will find yourself in places in the company of the wrong people, where you will be presented with more such opportunities.

Then you may even hear yourself complaining about why you keep making the same mistakes or why you keep falling for similar types or why you find yourself at the wrong places at the wrong time. Why?

Well, go out there and ask someone who learned from their mistake and decided not to repeat it anymore. Ask someone who decided not to be a loser again. Or ask someone how they manage to be at the right place at the right time. Just ask.

The difference between the right and wrong choice is never crystal clear when we are not awake at that moment. So, when we are not awake, why does it seem like the choices we make come back to bite us? If we are not awake, is it the darkness that seizes its chance to steal your light, when you doze off? Perhaps the darkness seduces you when you turn off your senses. It is like climbing up a tree with your eyes closed, not knowing which branch you are stepping on or whether it will be sturdy enough to carry you or not.

Is it about taking chances then? Is it about testing your limits of endurance? What if the branch you chose to step on breaks? What if the promise you have been given breaks?

What if your heart breaks?

Then, we should at least try to understand why we attempt to climb trees in the dark or fall for promises or choose tightropes to walk on. We should take responsibility for the fall we've taken, especially when we've managed to manifest it all by ourselves.

Some trips we take can literally deliver us to our favorite places. Some trips can cause us to fall. The ones we might remember best are those ones where we are the screenwriter, producer, director, lead actor, and audience. There is no fall like the one you set up all by yourself, for yourself. Irresponsibility is a great friend of carelessness. Together, they live in the house of immortality. They drink the juice of cruelty and eat the cake of nefariousness.

Your friends can also contribute significantly to your decision-making process. If you hang around with an irresponsible friend, it is likely you are careless. When you two are together, you will likely create an opportunity to make an immoral decision. The juice or cruelty will be your choice of substance abuse, and the cake of nefariousness you eat will be none other than the rest of your life filled with humility.

Because you are an energetic being, never stop checking in with your physical body before making a decision. Listen to your heart, consider your options, think again, do your research, and listen.

This is your life. You need to remember that you should be careful with it, as it can break easily. It is the tree you need to water. Although it is shared, your life is your responsibility. The goodness you do and the licentious trips you take set the path for you. Depending on your destination, your path can take you to the darkness or the light. Take a look around, read more, and listen without any judgment to those who have taken those trips before.

We all have stories. Yours can lighten up someone else's journey.

29

THE FRUIT OF EMPTINESS

IN THE EMPTINESS of life, sometimes you can lose the ability to use your senses. You may not see the beauty around you or hear your music. Your body might remain untouched, nothing tastes good, you can't smell the flowers, and you may feel like you've been forced to harvest things you don't have. Nothingness is all you are left with.

Even the number zero represents a code. Even nothingness itself has something in it. The ability to find something to hold onto while you are falling is embedded in all of us. We still fall, however, because we never activate that ability. When you do not have faith in yourself, you will not believe there is something inside you to hold onto.

When there seems to be too much going on in your life, your emptiness will grow. Challenges and struggles will overflow your cup. You think you have been given such an unfair amount of suffering that you cannot move anymore. You get lost in your emptiness. You look at your empty hands and your empty heart, your empty couch and eyes, and you believe that you have nothing. You feel like a child who has aged prematurely and lost your kite along with your hopes.

Does emptiness exist? Is it true? Do you really have nothing?

When you feel like you have nothing, you become the victim of your playful, bored mind. You forget all the goodness you have in you. You externalize your thoughts and rely on your perceptions alone. When you only look outside yourself, you only see what you are comfortable seeing, and you believe that what you see is true.

How about looking *within* yourself?

Nobody is empty inside. None of us are created empty. There is always extra water inside us when we feel parched and enough heat in our hearts when we feel cold. We are equipped with skills and the will to survive. But when your mind deceives you, it will feel like you have nothing. You can lessen the mind's power by remaining calm.

When you hear a voice within saying you have nobody supporting you, you should say, "I am here." When you find yourself being lonely, you should say, "I am here."

Meet with yourself when everything feels empty. Spend some time with yourself. Think about how you notice the emptiness. Sometimes, you will not see anyone in front of you and not a single being next to you. It will feel lonely. Then you will turn around and see that everyone is indeed behind you.

Some journeys should be completed alone. Some roads should be traveled alone. Some bitter fruit should be eaten alone. Some emptiness should be felt alone. Even then, you are not alone. You are just a bit ahead. Turn around and see how far you have traveled.

We should all look back every now and then. Not to feel sorry for ourselves or compare things to how beautiful life was back then, but to see the roads we have traveled. **Our experiences in this life contain tickets to our wisdom.** Do not throw your experiences away. The good ones will continue to make you feel good. The not-so-good ones, however, will be lessons for your awakening.

If you are not ready to wake up, then your experiences will be nothing but dust in the wind.

Your existence in this life is proof enough that miracles do happen. Things occur in life that human logic cannot comprehend.

Why would we even think the emptiness is here to stay? Why would you feed that thought? Nothing is permanent, so why should your feeling of emptiness be? When life challenges you, know that you are being invited to show what you are made of. Are you going to throw in the towel? Are you going to say, "I am done! Take me back."? Do you even know what might be waiting for you on the other side? Do we even know if there *is* indeed another side?

The other side is here already. Everything you live has another side. Every decision you make has another side. Every word you use has other meanings for those who hear it, depending on their current state of mind. You can say one thing and they can receive something else on their end. Where is *your* side then? If you feel empty, what do you think the other side of emptiness is? If you fall, what is the other option to that? If you are lonely, what is the alternative to it?

Do you remember the chapter when we talked about being in the company of two-way mirrors? You are your own "other side." In your existence, you have already been traveling between these sides. You have been exposed to many emotions, each of which has a twin. One life dwells in its diabolical headquarters, while the other volunteers to keep your heart clean, expecting nothing in return.

When you realize that sadness is falling on you like rain in November, what do you think you will feel? Because of your situation, the universe of emotions will deliver a message just before you lose yourself in your feeling of choice. The message will read:

> *Attention, twins! Another human being is about to go into downward spiral and will likely fall and break. So, who is interested in this?*

Remember, we cannot have two conflicting feelings within our bodies at the exact same time. So, either you pick one of the twins to arrive or they will take turns without even warning you.

Welcome to the possibility of giving birth to your bipolarity. While you are just a few seconds away from becoming the perfect host to your feeling of choice, the auction at the universe of emotions is about to end.

And the auctioneer goes, "Sold! Although the human being is

exposed to sadness already, this opportunity was purchased by envy and his twin, benevolence. Off you go. Enjoy!"

Meanwhile, on Earth, your sadness opens the door to envy and benevolence. It says, "This one is fifty-fifty. I comforted him for a little. You know I am always available for these beings. They keep me very busy. But he is yours now. Enjoy."

You look out the window. Although it is a beautiful Sunday morning in July and children are playing in the street, you don't even notice that your sadness is about to leave your body. Who do you think will knock on the door first?

Here we go. You hear a knock on the door, and envy walks in. It rubs your shoulders as you sit in your corner of the boxing ring.

Envy keeps encouraging you, shouting in your head, "Come on! Look at those people out there. They have nothing to worry about. They are having a splendid time. But you are all cooped up here and suffering. They are in such good company, but you are alone. It is too sunny for you, but they are soaking up the sun."

In less than a minute, you feel caged in and cannot break free. Envy is running the show now, and there is no room left for any other feeling in your body. You are hooked. While you still feel down, you do not hear the doorbell of your heart. You are too consumed with envy to invite in anything else.

However, the light never stops sponsoring your wellbeing. In the middle of your despair, it orchestrates a brilliant move. You hear that bell, and when you open the door, all the children are looking at you with such innocent faces. They all start to speak in desperation.

"Mister! Mister! Please, Mister. Our kite got stuck in the big tree in your yard. Please, Mister. Help us. Please."

You struggle at first, because, now, benevolence is on your heart's doorstep, too. It still is a beautiful day outside as you leave your house and step into your garden. You look at the big, old maple tree and notice the red kite.

Not willingly, you start to climb the tree. You see the initials you carved on the very same tree when you were a little kid, the same age as the ones waiting below for you to rescue their kite. You also remember the feeling of when your father helped you get *your* kite down once from the same maple tree.

A sense of kindness fills your heart. Envy goes back to the auction house. You retrieve the kite safely and recognize the gratitude in the kids' eyes. You become their hero, just like your dad was to you. You remember the magical summer day your father introduced you to kindness.

When an opportunity arises, emotions will take advantage of it. You need to know, though, you are still the gatekeeper. You either open the door or you don't. If you do open it, do not hurry to invite any solicitor selling something in your home. You need to know you have a right to say no. Instead, start to practice saying something like this:

"I notice I am feeling envious. I acknowledge that."

That's it. However, you don't have to analyze it to make it fit your theories. Do not create stories around it. If you do, you will be bewitched by your own storytelling ability. It is okay to feel it, but do not get attached to it.

Do not put yourself down, either, when you believe you have wasted time investing in such emotions. There are no right or wrong feelings. They don't have to be labeled as good or bad. They are there for you to decide what your choice will be. It is like an all-you-can-eat buffet. Too much consumption of anything can give you a stomach ache.

Do not stay in those emotions for a long time, because there are plenty of them everywhere already. There will always be enough for you to pick from. The ones you label as bad can teach you so much about life. The ones you label as good can do the same. But what can be found in the middle of your journey going through these emotions?

You can get your answer when you are not attached to either side of the emotion. Just accept them as they are. There is a reason they have showed up. Do not stay in that state of mind for so long.

If you want to visit the one who is looking at you on the other side of the two-way mirror, do not worry about having to travel far, because it is only a deep breath away.

Next time, when you focus on your life being empty, at least leave the door open for life's magic to arrive. **The feeling of**

emptiness is an invitation for you to start coloring the pages of your book of life. That means your child-self is begging you to go out and fly your kite—go to a park and swing a little and not worry about getting your shoes dirty. Just go out and play in the puddles for a while.

Feeling empty can be a blessing. It is telling you that you are not giving one hundred percent to your own life. It is facing you directly and challenging you to do something with your life. It is encouraging you to get creative. It is telling you about being fierce. It is showing you postcards from places you have never visited. It is kicking you in your rear because it is the high time for you to do something for yourself and use your gift to make this world a better place for all living beings.

Emptiness is your opportunity to fill. What would you like to fill it with? Get eccentric a little bit. Break your chains.

30

EMBROIDERING YOUR BRUISES

HAVE YOU EVER known someone with a broken heart? Have you ever noticed what brokenhearted people have in common? They feel they have lost their freedom to fly and land on other hearts again. Their heartache turns their sadness into fetters, and their pain seems unerasable. When someone's heart breaks, it feels like their wings are broken, too. Some spend the rest of their lives trying to forget their pain. Some let their hopes seep through the fissures in their fractured hearts.

Can a broken heart be put back together? When it is torn, can it be stitched entirely? Can the wounds be forgotten as though they had never existed?

Why were we created with such a soft part of ourselves? It is protected by our ribcage, as if it is a precious golden bird. Is that to prevent it from escaping? Or from getting damaged?

When it seems like your heart escapes you, some things become more apparent. The light in your eyes, the spirited child within you, the joy you have accumulated, the smile on your face, the fierceness of your curiosity, and your reasons to be happy will also leave with your heart. But your wings will still be there. Nothing can break those. If you want to fly back to memories or search for your vanished heart, use your wings. Rise above.

You have the ability to heal your bruises. You will witness your own strength as you dig yourself out of the tar of heavy pain. As you dig yourself out of the drama, you will also wash away the tar that once glued your wings shut. Then life will return to your veins, even if your heart resists pumping blood back through your body. You will get up and hold your heart in your hands. You will not ignore the bruises. You will touch each crack in it every night and learn to keep it safe in your ribcage. You will find the strength to look at yourself in the mirror, and someday you will see the light in your eyes return. You will learn to listen to sad songs again without falling apart. One day, you will notice the change in your heartbeat. Maybe slowly at first, but you *will* start to hear your heart's music.

There will come a time when your bruises will be more than just yellow and purple. They will generate more colors, and the cracks in your damaged heart will turn into rivers carrying many wonderful colors created by your bruises. Your creativity for life will start to design lessons learned on your heart: a fantastic art piece will be embroidered on your heart. It will be so vibrant, it can be seen from anywhere by anyone.

The love you have learned will be shared. Living beings will come to you as they recognize the purity in your heart.

Your heart is your art. Paint it freely with love, kindness, and compassion.

Your bruises are the rivers of survival carried on the healing currents of life. You will surrender your pain once the rivers reach the ocean of forgiveness. In that ocean, there are so many shades of blue, you will no longer cling to your own state of feeling blue. At the moment when the sky meets the water, you will cease to think that you were once abandoned. The elements of life will build you back up. You will start to regenerate yourself piece by piece, and in each piece will be a great deal of space to write your new stories.

Even at night, when the owls listen to your stories and the moon brightens your room, you will still feel the energy of the water that brings you back to life. You will cover yourself with a blanket made of love, and you will fall asleep with music in your heart. Fireflies will chase your nightmares away, and moths will bring you light from every porch and streetlight they visit. Your embroidered heart will continue to play music, and the fairies of the forests will dance to celebrate your return.

Coming back to life with a broken heart is a journey we take that seems difficult even to start. The road in front of us is paved by our sorrow and will be washed with tears of despair. The memories of every lost soul on their own journey will walk in front of us, as if they want us to follow them to the other side of life.

You may consider following them, hoping it will end your sorrow and not realizing that ending yours in that fashion will initiate sorrow for those you leave behind. Walking on that road takes courage. You may get tricked by the street performers of the dark, who may try to impress your hollow eyes. Although they are after your broken heart, they will disguise themselves as the painkillers of the light.

Then you will see someone just like yourself, who is collecting colors from the flowers by the pond. As she starts to paint over her bruises, you will remember your own cuts. She sees you crying and notices you do not see the swans around you. She gets your attention and shows you one swan who is offering you her feather. The feather is your sign. Its lightness represents your option to rise above. The pain in your heart does not have to stay there forever. For every fallen person's broken heart, there will always be feathers to be found.

You can choose to embroider your bruises. **Having a broken heart is okay**. Being afraid of its incompleteness is okay because, in this life, there will be ups and downs. Remember: when you fall, it is okay to get up. It is okay to learn from your sorrow and start to paint with the bruises in your heart.

Just remember that healing doesn't happen alone. There is always help around us, even if it seems to be unseen.

31

NOSTRUM FOR HARUM-SCARUM

CAN ABSENTMINDEDNESS be cured? Should it be?

Where is the mind located anyway? How do you approach someone who acts like he is all over the place? Would you just let them be? Probably you would, until he starts to annoy you.

There is a way to keep the mind within the body. Is there a way for us to keep our thoughts to ourselves? Would we still survive, if we chose to listen?

Silence is an excellent way to hear the messages of your body. Think about how we spend most of our days. Do you seriously spend time listening to your body? The mind wants to run all over the place, not noticing the traffics. A mind that lacks wisdom will push you in front of a car on a busy highway.

The mind yearns for surprises and looks for any opportunity to use your energy. It is like children having a sleepover at your house: they are never too tired to go to sleep. You eavesdrop on their conversation just to make sure everything is okay. You hear them talking about the letter "A," and then jump to the letter 'K," and then every other letter of every other language of the world. As if it is impossible to stop, they cannot give up talking. Then, in the middle of your sleep, you realize you don't hear anyone. You get up and check on them. You find them all passed out, sleeping in the most impossible positions, because they were exhausted.

The mind works like that. It chatters five hundred miles a minute until your body cannot take it anymore. Perhaps the body controls the mind, too, instead of the mind seeming to control everything. If you can manage to keep the mind within the physical limitations of the body, you will see that, eventually, you will be able to quiet the mind.

When the mind is calm, the emotions lose their effectiveness. They can no longer make you feel good or bad. They become just like bubbles in the air: they arrive and they leave. They show up and they pop. They appear and then they disappear. Your mind cannot rescue itself from your calmness. You keep acknowledging what is happening while being silent.

However, you do not tell your mind to go and check out what is going on. You do not instruct your mind to do detective work. The second you do that, it will already be too late. Your mind will start to do the detective work, and it will find a hundred more cases just like the first one. It will write about each instance's family tree, and then, on the way back, it will alert you that you are hungry, but it will let you wonder what you feel like eating. And when the "feeling" gets invited back, you really are in trouble. You have to start calming yourself down again.

The good news is you can get better at practicing calming the mind. Unfortunately, many of us are not good at that. It is as if we are slaves to our minds and also their number-one ally.

Can you break free? Can you instruct your mind to take a vacation?

Can you learn to live in the moment without being attached to anything? If you can do that, you will not be interested in what your mind brings back from your past or what possible ways it tricks you to draw you into the future. It is like playing ball with your dog: no matter how far you throw it, your dog will find it and bring it back to you. Your mind says, "Master! Look what I found while I was looking for the ball. Did you not lose this when you were five years old? And do you remember how upset your mother was? Did she even tell you why she treated you like that…?" You know where this story is going, right?

If you want to end the agony, you say, "Good boy," and the game is over. Or you can say, "Tell me more," and let the new phases of suffering begin.

If your mind is still chattering, you are still in the game. As long as you are willing to play, the mind will not stop playing, either.

Try this right now. Take a deep breath, and count while you inhale. Then count again while you exhale. When you try to be calm, your mind does not stop fetching the ball. But when you count while you are breathing, you give your mind its "job," something to do. It's just like telling your dog, "After getting this ball, run all the way to the end of the universe, and count how many minutes it takes."

That will keep him busy.

When a thought shows up, you still have the power to send it back. You do not have to own it and invest in it. If you experience being overwhelmed by receiving unwanted emails in your inbox, you might understand this subject better. You can either open and go through all of the junk emails, you can organize them, or you can delete them. One of the biggest mistakes you can make is opening an email containing a virus that can crash your program. The same logic goes for your thoughts, too. Some thoughts contain the virus. The moment you decide to elaborate on that viral thought, there will be worms crawling out of the can you just opened.

Those thoughts follow a diabolical hierarchy. Once they are activated, it can get tough to interrupt their chain of command. However, the process can be interrupted. You can choose to stop investing in a viral thought. The tricky part hides, knocking on your door with innocent inquiries.

You cannot identify each viral thought right away, especially if you are sleepwalking. It can sneak into your system when you are not aware. Once in, the next thing they do is drag in their offspring. Before you know it, you are feeding its grandchildren. When it starts to consume you to the point where you can't think about anything else, your life will be controlled by your shadow. You still need to remember that nothing is permanent and you can change the way you think. The virus does not have to spread.

Remember: you are in control. And the thought that contains a virus will not reveal its contents. It can, however, try to trespass in your garden of intuition. That is when your body gets the alarm. It senses there is an intruder trying to break your harmony and alter your peace.

Unfortunately, not everyone pays attention to their internal warning device. Viral thoughts are seductive and flirtatious. **Those of us who are careless will be bewitched by the instant ecstasy created by a forbidden thought**. Those of us who are bored may trifle with its intriguing invitation.

The remedy for carelessness is mindfulness.

Before a viral thought is invited, after its brief introduction, you need to take a deep breath and say, "I embrace your visit, but I am not interested in handing my house over to you."

You do not have to invest in every thought. Focus on the ones that are uplifting; loving, kind, and compassionate. Start caring more. You will realize you can tame your thoughts. Choose consciously. **You can train your thoughts**. Just like building muscles through exercise and practice, you can create a healthier thought process, too. You will see that the time you spend on a viral thought becomes shorter, once you become more mindful. Eventually, these thoughts will linger outside of your mind. If you do not open the door, they will not be able to come in.

Choose your thoughts carefully. Regardless how small a thought might be, it can either manifest more darkness or more light. You are in control.

32

NOXIOUS CHOICES

SOME CHOICES WE MAKE can be toxic. They are like double-edged swords: they can cut both you and the ones around you.

When it comes to the moment of making a choice, try to take a deep breath before rushing into it. What you do, in that moment of choosing, will create a path. Your energy will form your intention, and your intention will either lighten up your path or darken it.

Your path is not hidden from you but becomes difficult to see, when it is not lit. In the dark, you can't read the contract you are signing. Offering you the contract is like a pernicious merchant selling a lifetime of vinegar labeled as honey. It will seem like the deal of the century, and, in your sleepy state of mind, you will purchase the vinegar, believing you have just bought honey, instead. With that transaction, you will cripple yourself and isolate others.

Signing a contract in the dark is what happens when you make a decision out of anger, resentment, or any other state of mind where your ill nature is running the show. Your harvest will be ill, too. The food you make out of your harvest will be noxious. You will consume the poison of unmindfulness but will not be aware of its speed, as it covers your existence while you are sleepwalking.

Being unmindful is carelessness, a medal you never want to wear around your neck. **Carelessness is what turns off the lights on your path and sucks you into the darkness.** Make sure that you care. If you do nothing else in any given moment, at least try to pay attention to your thoughts and your words.

Even if we do not see it, there is an alliance of lights created by the mindfulness of those who care. Every time you care, you contribute to the fund that creates more light. There are light-workers all around us, and they never give up. They see someone crying and become a shoulder for them to cry on. They see someone who has fallen and become wings for him. They do not judge, and they do not seek any recognition. They share what they have. When you are hungry, they are not full. They believe we all are in this together. Light-workers care and will not give up on you.

When you arrived on this planet, the chip of a light-worker had already been embedded in you. However, you were also given multiple backstage passes to the party hosted by the Earth's rancorous citizens. You really are free to do whatever you want to do with your free will. Some of us activate the chip to continue our lives as light-workers, while some of us use the free pass to become the hypnotized slaves of the vitriolic.

Sometimes, there will be opportunities for the rancorous to go to the light; there are also traps for light-workers to fall into the darkness. These experiences are critical. Once you learn that obscurity prevents you from meeting your true self, you may want to take advantage of the opportunity to become a light-worker. Now, why would a light-worker fall into a trap created by the darkness?

As humans, we all fall at least once in our lifetime. Do not assume that your life cannot take an unexpected turn. Anyone's life can change without warning. Somedays, we can taste the sweetness of success but also smell the disturbing fumes of failures. However, **our success in life will be more than our failures as long as we don't fall back into a careless state of mind and continue to sleepwalk.**

It is a very special occasion when a light-worker falls into the darkness. Do you remember the part about the Human Resources

Division of the Darkness? When they identify an excellent candidate, they will do anything to get that special light-worker into their department.

It takes one good deed, any form of kindness or one true moment of compassion, to get someone from the darkness into the light. However, taking that special light-worker into the darkness requires an army of slaves of the darkness to orchestrate the best opus of their existence. And they will do it.They will send messages to every dimension of every dark energy in life to trap that special light-worker.

They will plan, they will write, they will design the stage, they will hire the players, and they will set up the light-worker. They will not give up. They will pursue. But why would the light allow the darkness to trip their special light-worker to fall into such trap?

Because, in the beginning, before their arrival as humans, everyone gets screened for their potential. Some will score so high that the darkness and the light will strongly want that person on their team. That person's free will is the only deciding factor that places him either in the house of darkness or the house of light. After his final choice, neither side will totally let him go.

Not many light-workers will be given an opportunity to fall into the darkness. But if they fall, it can create so much wisdom that not only will they secure their place in the light, but they will lift up many other fallen ones, too. It takes a special soul to fall into the darkness from the light. Their suffering cannot be handled by many others. These souls have to go through a journey where they meet rulers of the darkness and their believers.

At first, a light-worker will not be able to forgive himself for falling from grace. At some point, feeling weak in his loneliness, he will think about giving up. His isolation will become anxiety and claustrophobia as he worries about being abandoned by the light. He will question the light's loyalty. He will face losing his faith in the light, because he will see how the darkness has been gathering all its forces to pull him deeper into the darkness but thinks the light seems to be doing nothing to help him. He will assume that the light chose to support his being sacrificed.

The darkness and the light have an agreement. In the rare event when a particular light-worker falls into the darkness, because it is not their field, the light cannot interfere until the light-worker starts to see a glimpse of light again by restoring his faith in himself. Therefore, the light can only observe the first round. But it is still there. It will not leave the light-worker behind, as there is always hope for fallen ones to find the light, when they are lost.

The first round is the most difficult for the fallen light-worker. He will be tested. He will be thrown into his nightmares. He will cry and drown in his sadness. His heartache will shatter his joy. He will lose his interest in life and the things he used to enjoy. He will continue to feed his guilt, and whenever he wants to sleep, his regret will share his pillow with him. He will feel like a lion without fangs, an eagle without eyes, and a dolphin without joy. He will sink deeper every time he believes the light is so far away. He will lose his appetite and pack his dreams into his luggage, but he will know he will not be traveling to the places where his broken heart can teach him how to love himself again.

The first round will not reveal the results he desperately needs to see. The darkness will start to celebrate its victory. Having such a spectacular soul with so much love and compassion will certainly help the darkness to win the eternal war. The darkness will believe it can now defeat the light, using their new recruit, as the light-worker's eyes start to grow dim.

As the light-worker starts to fall asleep, his body will become colder. His summer will turn into winter. His spring will run out of green, and his autumn will forget to change its colors. Life will start to lose its meaning. He will start smiling less and breathing more heavily. He will no longer receive letters, and no more music will be delivered to his doorstep. His loneliness will grow in his shrinking, bruised heart.

The darkness sends messages through the wolves, so they lift their heads and start to howl about their imminent victory. Dark witches will start to brew their revenge in the cauldron of animosity, adding a touch of hatred and some anger as they continue their brewing. They will pour in some frustration and resentment, too, making sure their vengeance tastes as dark as their soul. Finally, they will head off to steal the last thing they need to finish brewing their soup. At the darkest hour of the darkest night, they will visit the fallen light-worker, who will be only half alive.

The light-worker will linger on the thin bridge between life and death. He will see the emptiness of his past as he thinks about all the gifts he has thrown away. The hyenas of the darkness will come closer with their peace offering. They will hand him a promise wrapped in life's unseen sin. The light-worker will try to burn the journal of his failure by looking to find something to start his fire.

The darkness will be so eager to recruit him, it will bring a flame from a place across from heaven. When they hand him hell's fire to burn his journal of failures, the light-worker will see something in the flame. First, his hope will start to burn and then his faith. The dark witches will be ready for their feast of eternal victory. Hyenas' stomachs will start to sing the songs of the light-worker's agony.

In the middle of his burning, the light-worker will recognize what he has seen in the fire. As he turns into ash, his soul will rise with the firelight. He will get up and start the second round.

Better understanding his situation, he will say to himself, "If the darkness sent all their forces to take me, then I must represent the light. All this suffering I have been going through was never meant to destroy me. My suffering is my gift, an opportunity to learn from."

The darkness will leave the stage unwillingly. The light will take over, as there will be no round three.

33

SIMPLETON'S CAPTIVITY

WOULD YOU BE offended if you were asked whether you had ever done anything stupid in your life? If you say no, do you think anyone will believe you?

If your stupidity holds you captive, learn to be thankful, regardless how long that takes to do. Your new life journey will be built on the priceless foundation of your stupidity. That means your life is not over when you make a mistake.

When you continue your life as if nothing has happened, however, you will not learn your lesson. If you're ecstatic because you acted stupidly, you will not learn your lesson. If any type of blaming or finger-pointing comes into the picture, you will not learn your lesson.

Let your foolishness hold you captive for awhile. During your loss of freedom, allow yourself to see your life from a different perspective. You may become the target of firey arrows heading your way, and you should know that some of those arrows will hit you. They will hurt and burn you, too. Those arrows will unzip your shiny armor, and you will be naked, trying to hide in your humiliation. You will be criticized and judged. You will be isolated and exiled in your own garden of disillusionment. You will let your garden go and weeds will take over. But those weeds will become dandelions, teaching you to see them as flowers of resistance. They will find a way to come back.

You need to find your own way to come back to life and build happiness after sorrow and disappointments. There will always be signs of hope all around you. The seen and the unseen will help you to see signs, even while you are in captivity. What kind of thing or person would be interested in taking a fool hostage? Why? How can a fool learn a lesson?

If your weakness can be used against you, would it be beneficial for you to expose that to your enemy? The darkness loves to gorge itself on a fool's weakness for temptation; it will not stop testing you. If you cannot discipline yourself, anything you crave or desire can be used to lure you into captivity. Basically, you will build your own prison and stay in it, while assuming you are free.

When we chase after our desires, we usually don't notice they are carrots dangling by the darkness. When we are only interested in seeing one thing—what we desire—are we be able to see anything else? Do we risk missing things happening around us when we are held captive by our desires? The imbalance we experience in the world, unfortunately, manifests at an individual level. When we consume more than we need, we affect the frequency of life. Desire will keep your mind busy; your need for something may never lessen. As long as you are interested in getting or having *more*, the universe will provide you with more. But more of what?

Fool's captivity has no walls or boundaries. He is only concerned with getting satisfied. The need for satisfaction is his weakness. Once his weakness is discovered, he will be captured effortlessly.

However, if a human's craving is satisfied only by material things, it can only be temporary. Soon, the mind starts sending signals for cravings once again. A cycle is created: desire turns into satisfaction then satisfaction becomes boredom and boredom awaken desire again. Your life turns into a prison that remains active due to your foolish absentmindedness.

When desire takes center stage in a careless mind, ask yourself where that desire is coming from, especially when you don't need what you seem to want so desperately. Dig deeper into this, because you will realize that somewhere in that bag of reasons is a package called "boredom." This can be an eye-opener for you, if you choose to understand it further.

Boredom is not having enough courage to admit you are pursuing your life as a victim. Also, that you are lazy.

Do not be a permanent fool. Live your life fully. There are more ways to find bliss than by chasing after your desires. The weaknesses you have can be turned into strengths. When you are mindful, foolishness is nothing but a word. In this life, we are all subject to entrapment, but you do not have to be the fool who builds his own trap because he wants some cheese.

Learn to listen to your desires, but you don't have to act on them. Thoughts of desire may come to you, but you don't have to feed them. Try to find the root cause of your boredom, instead.

34

EXCAVATING THE VOID

WHEN THERE IS nothing left to comprehend, what do you think happens? When you think you have nothing left to give, do people start asking less from you? Does the world stop spinning because you feel empty inside?

When all you have left is the void, what do you do? If all you see is a big emptiness and you believe you have nothing to fill it with, should you give up trying?

Why don't you try to get into that void and start looking around a bit? The void itself takes up space. And that space may well be between you and someone else. The unused spaces between people are empty spaces waiting to be occupied. So, do not go around it. Get inside of it.

It's just like when you look for a stud on your wall to hang a picture. Do the same thing: tap gently on the walls of your void. Once you hear a solid sound instead of a hollow one, start to drill in. Continue drilling a hole within the void big enough that it turns into a tunnel. Use this tunnel to get to the other end of the void. Take a look around and realize that even voids have secret passages waiting to be discovered. All the loneliness around us grows greater by the distances we create. What are we afraid of?

The world we live in does not get any bigger in size, yet the world's population has been steadily increasing. Isn't it amazing that there is so many of us who are lonely? But the loneliness cannot be due to the number of beings who occupy the same space. It is internal, too, not just something created externally. Loneliness is also our own doing. We should not blame anyone else for our own voluntary exile.

If the situation you are in is not satisfying for you, what should you do? Sit and wait, hoping someone or something will eventually change the situation? Or get up and start doing something about it?

Get up! Do not let your exile become the very last part of your existence. Start getting to know yourself, including all the beauty and ugliness you have. Look at all your beauty marks and deep scars, and whatever you have, just accept it. Then sit down and think about whatever it is that is holding you back. Your life's success cannot be measured by your physical beauty. When your soul is suffering, your eyes cannot hold a smile. When your spirit is broken, your beautiful body cannot follow the steps of any dance. Just like loneliness, emptiness can also be internal. Exile, failure, disappointment, guilt, regret, deception, beauty, and ugliness are all internal.

Can we build a bridge between the unfilled dreams of our faraway escapes and our disappointed selves? When everything seems to be dying inside, how do we let others around us know? We cannot afford to be too clueless and assume we can solve our internal struggles by ourselves all the time.

Our internalized labels are the product of our perception of external exchanges. Sometimes, we get caught in the war of misunderstood intentions over our fruitless attempts. The burden of our self-destruction becomes heavier to carry. **It takes courage to claim responsibility for the bridges we have burned between the world and ourselves**. But when we try to survive our unbearable loneliness, how can we find the hope to invite courage?

Thoughts can easily be internalized when we believe we are their owners. We are also the receiver, the cultivator, the carrier, the housekeeper, and the transparent host. We are part of the collective. Our connection to one another is energetic and cannot be clearly defined with words. The more personal spaces we create, the more heavily we will suffer in our loneliness.

We cannot feed the void through external vehicles. It should not be ignored as though its emptiness means nothing. Other people may be able to sense the void in you, but you are the only one who knows how it feels. Although you should not try to internalize everything, there are still endless opportunities for anyone who is willing to look within themselves.

So, get closer to that void of yours. Is it trying to tell you something? Or is it getting bigger every time you choose to escape from yourself? Are you the maker of your void? When your emptiness starts to spread to the corners of your world, where can you go that does not feel empty? The fear of losing what you have can perhaps be the very thing you need to wake up.

Recognizing your emptiness is a promising start to your self-discovery. However, it is only the start. Your homework's completion will depend on your commitment to healing. What could be better than having that emptiness when you exercise your creativity? You will have a blank canvas in front of you. Your paint will be everything you want to do. Your color selection is limitless. Nobody can hold you back. You can paint any season you want and use any color you want. Your emptiness could be the gift you find wrapped inside yourself.

Open yourself up and start to enjoy what you are seeing. Start being thankful for what you have. There is so much you can do with your life. Feeling empty is just your internal warning device telling you that you are not living your life to its fullest potential.

Feeling empty inside means you are cheating on your true self for not showing up to your life.

35

ABANDONED DREAMS

ABANDONED DREAMS live in the haunted chambers of your heart. They become the ghost of your untimely death within your living body. Closing your eyes will not make them go away. They cannot be forgotten or ignored.

Forsaken dreams will never stop speaking to you. Regardless of how tightly you close your eyes to avoid facing them, you cannot escape seeing them. Your dreams are a part of you, and you cannot continue to ignore part of your existence. They are the fuel for your engine. They are the air you breathe. When you abandon them, you also give up on yourself. They are equipped with loyalty, as they live in your veins. They carry blood to your heart and always ask with curiosity, "Is today the day that he will make us a reality?"

These dreams will continue to remind you of this with persistence. When you wake up, they will ask. When you sleep, they will ask. Although your dreams will never give up on you, your mind, body, and soul may stop keeping them alive. That is when you have accepted the idea of letting them go. But nobody truly lets go of their dreams. They may become buried under the chores of our daily lives. They may be put on the shelves of pawn shops in the hope that you will retrieve them someday. They may remain on the unwritten pages of that book you always wanted to write. They may be abandoned on the streets of cities you never have a chance to visit. They may get trapped within the smell of flowers you never plant.

However, abandoned dreams bear witness to our unsatisfied lives when we are trying to figure out what's missing in them.

How can your life be complete when you are not in it?

How can your dreams come true when you are away from them?

Take a moment and think about those who still openly confess the dreams they have left behind. Listen to their stories. We all have stories. Although we were taught to follow our dreams, most of us continue to have reasons for not pursuing our dreams.

We often get too busy to stop and look at who is behind us. If you knew your little child had been following you everywhere you go, calling your name and begging for your attention then asking you to pick her up, would you continue to ignore her? Would you leave her behind because you have other things to do? Would your child even make it onto your to-do list, let alone your bucket list? So stop the insanity of living in the rat race, hoping that, as soon as you collect your medals, you will pay attention to your dreams.

When you find yourself stuck in the rat race, stop for a minute and just look behind you. It is your dream that has been following you. It is your dream that believes you will take it with you wherever you are going.

How about you? Have you been too busy and preoccupied with your rat race to take your dreams with you? Do you think people with foresaken dreams look happy? Even if they believe they have accomplished everything they wanted in their lives, they still won't be able to hide their sadness when their unanswered dreams become the topic of conversation. Just observe them. Ask those individuals that particular question. Most people will have great answers for you. Some of us may not be able to pick up our dreams because we become supporters of our loved ones' dreams. Their dreams come true through their loved ones. Those parents' hearts will ache as they support their children's dreams coming true, but not their own.

Do not take your life for granted. Do not assume you will get back to making your dreams a reality only when you think the time is right, because the time you think will be the right one may never knock at your door.

You came to this life not really knowing much about yourself. Your dreams begin to grow as you say your first word and take your first step. You dream of the seven seas and all the wonders of the world. What do you think you actually do when you abandon your dreams?

Think again. **Every time you abandon your dreams, you actually leave behind the child within you**. And when you do that, you are indeed abandoning the possibility of finding your truth. So what and who is the child within? When we grow older, we carry in our spirit another passenger on the journey called life. Most adults seem to have long forgotten their childhood dreams or simply do not want to talk about them. Your child-self is invisible to those who are not looking. However, they know the child has been there all along.

The child within will find a way to get your attention and remind you that you are off track. It will not rest until it is acknowledged. Imagine, when you were a little child, you wanted to be an astronaut. Maybe some people around you supported your dream, and maybe some people thought you were only dreaming. Let's say, as you grew older, your life took you to a path that had nothing to do with traveling to outer space and visiting other planets. Although you have never forgotten about your dream, you have never brought it up, either, because you've already built a life far away from being an astronaut.

People sometimes think that those childhood dreams are just dreams and that reality is not built on such dreams.

Wrong!

It all starts with imagination. That is the key. And if you think that child within will not kick your heart every time you think of the stars, space ,and the planets, you must still be sleeping.

Dreams are like shadows except they can make themselves be seen at any time of the day, even in the dark. Any dream you once had but have not yet manifested does not have to turn into a ghost or zombie to chase you. Some dreams have a special space in your heart. You know what they are. When you think of those dreams, you hear a silent cry in your heart. Perhaps a tear rolls down your cheek. Those dreams never leave your heart, and you know it.

Sometimes, we act as though we can move on with our lives perfectly well, even with the heaviness of our abandoned dreams. Moving forward may not mean much to some of us, especially when the void we carry is bigger than our success. Could our life really feel complete? When you leave part of you behind, can you actually be moving forward as a whole being?

You get to design your life, and you get to define your level of success. Others don't. Some of us do better keeping all their broken pieces together, but some of us fall into more pieces as we try to move forward. If you feel like you can no longer continue, perhaps you should take a break. Perhaps you should listen. Perhaps the child within has something to say.

36

WHY ARE YOU HERE, REALLY?

HAVE YOU EVER thought about finding an answer to the question above? I believe it would be a great experience to ask the occupants of this planet for their answers, no matter what language, and see if their culture, religion, location, lifestyle, and values have any effect on their thought process.

Some of us believe in the concept of "heaven and hell." Some of us believe there is such thing as "reincarnation." Some of us believe in angels, monsters, werewolves, vampires, aliens, fairies, and so on. Amazing, isn't it?

What do you believe? Do you know why you are here, on this earth?

Shouldn't we ask why we do not fully exercise our brain's capacity? What if we did? Would we able to figure out the reason for our existence?

It does not feel like we are alone in the universe. Perhaps we feel so helpless and bored, our imagination creates multiple scenarios. After all, we may think it is better to believe in something than to have faith in nothing. When things cannot be explained by our minds, they can be escalated somewhere else, in this case perhaps to a higher power. Do you believe that someone or something exists above any of its creatures?

The answers you get to these questions can be overwhelming. Some of us spend most of our lives trying to understand the meaning of life. Why were we born as humans, instead of as something else? So, the more you think about it, the faster you will go down the rabbit hole. Are you ready for it?

Imagine you are locked up. You cannot get out. You have lost your freedom. Every day is the same. To stay alive, you need to take care of yourself. Would you sit in your cell, doing nothing with your time but think about how you ended up in that situation, and repeat that process every day? What would you gain from that? Would you accept what is happening to you and figure out what you want to do with your days?

Life can also be a prison. When we think we are free, we may not be at all. First of all, your true self is never free, as long as you continue to believe you are what you think your identity is. It does not matter how much material wealth you have accumulated, without your overall health, you are not free. **When you hold on to anger all the time, you are not free.** Could you be serving a life sentence in the prison of your own making?

Most of us don't even realize we are not actually free. We are shackled by financial debt, suffocated in relationships we are not happy with, and serving our sentence working to earn a living by doing jobs that do not spark our hearts or build the joy we have forgotten.

How do we become free then, free from the thoughts that keep returning to our mind and we cannot seem to escape? **We are not free if we live our heads, dwelling on the past or the future.** We are not free if we are not content with what we have at that moment. We are not free if we feed envy. We are not free if we feed only our desires. We are not free when another being is haunted by the ghost of his suffering.

So, if you are not free in this life, does it even matter if we figure out the reasons for our being here? Could this life experience be designed so intelligently that it actually teaches us to be free? Is this life a sentence we have to serve or a school we have to attend with full commitment?

While we cluelessly float on the river of oblivion en route to this planet, do you think maybe we are told the reason for our journey as human beings in this world? Is it possible perhaps we come to this planet from somewhere else to learn so, when we go back, we can share the wisdom? **When you let your imagination fly effortlessly, you may see that the possibilities are endless**. You may end up losing your mind as you try to solve life's mystery. Also, knowing what's coming next can take away that excitement.

Once again, it will be up to you what you do with your life. Just make sure you are not wasting it. Regardless what your theory may be, there is still one thing that counts, and that is staying alive. The first thing about life's secret is **to stay alive**. However, there are many lives wasted around us, all because we take this incredible learning opportunity called *life* for granted.

Here is another dilemma. Why is it that we are so concerned about trying to get whatever we don't have? Are we trying to complete something? Are we part of a puzzle? Do we complete ourselves through shopping, education, relationships, family, travel, and mistakes? Could that be our purpose? To complete ourselves?

What about our true self? What is true self? How do you find it? Could it be our purpose to find whatever that true self might be? What if we have multiple purposes in this life? How do we choose which one to go after? How do you know which direction to go? If being alive is the first thing on the list, then **having the best version of your life** should be the next. Great! How many of us really know what the best version of our lives is? Do *you* know?

Are you the designer of your life? Or is your life designed by others, like society, religion, school, family, and friends? How about substance abuse? Who is the designer of your life?

Although this is just an observation, we all seem to be prone to making mistakes. We are emotional, we can be caring or careless, we can be mindful or absentminded, and we can be paralyzed by the number of paths presented to us. This planet is breathtakingly beautiful, yet it can also be savage because of us. Animals don't burn forests, but humans can. Whales do not poison the ocean, but humans have. Butterflies do not pollute the air, but humans do. How many different versions of human beings are being sent to this magical planet, with some determined to destroy it and some focused on sustaining its beauty? Why do some of us serve the darkness and some of us serve the light? Clearly it is not logical to think that we are all seeking the same purpose. What if someone's purpose is to create chaos and yours is to spread the peace? Where would the two of you meet in this life? On the bridge built between heaven and hell? Some believe that heaven and hell are already here, and we take our turns visiting them as we thrive within the limitations of being human. Have you ever been on that bridge?

There are so many bridges that we cross. Some take us to the light and some to the other side. However, not everyone who crosses a particular bridge comes back. The pain, sadness, ache, yearning, and suffering in any form is for us, as is comfort, peace, and calm. Love and joy are for us, too. When we are exposed to opposites, we become challenged by the choices we must make. It is not easy when both the darkness and the light are there for us.

Is life's purpose to allow us to choose which side we want to be part of? Is it going to be the darkness or the light? Do you have a reason for being here? If there *is* a reason, why do we have to figure it out on this planet? Have we actually signed up for human experience voluntarily? Or are we being forced to have one, instead? Since you are here now, what are you planning to do with your life?

Since we are already here, I suggest we make the best of it. Unfortunately, even when we think we are doing the right thing, sometimes we still trip and fall. That is also an experience some of us have never been able to get over. Would you blame and judge someone who no longer wants to have this experience? If life is so precious, why is it planted in the middle of a mine field?

Why are we here?

Did we choose this place willingly? Is life our homework? Are we to write an essay on it? After all those years, generation after generation, it still does not look like we have learned our lesson. Are we failing? If we are failing, are we disappointing ourselves? Or did we originate this game of survival?

Perhaps we are just like the pieces used in a game that is played between the darkness and the light. When one or the other captures you, you go to their team. This game perhaps has been played since the beginning of our existence.

This is our life. At the end of the day, when you are alone in your thoughts or when you reflect back on your day, do you go to sleep peacefully? Or with a big knot in your stomach? In this life, we are not the pieces of such games. Because of our free will, we do not have to participate in any games.

If you remember, I mentioned a list. The first thing on the list was "being alive." The second item was "having the best version of your life." The third thing should be "**stripping yourself of the identity you have been clinging to**."

When you let go of the identity, you may realize what or who your blank version may be. That revelation can help you to a fresh start, as you do not have to waste your energy proving who you think you are, instead of just being. Life can have many purposes. Awakening is important and necessary, since it is the way to your enlightenment. Maybe you are here to wake up. Maybe the world is the bed you have been sleeping in. Who is singing a lullaby to you?

Not everyone had had someone sing them a lullaby. There are those who have tasted the coldness of being homeless. There are those who have witnessed the collapse of their hopes. There are those out there destroying other beings' lives. There are those out there wasting food and water, knowing there are hungry, thirsty babies being washed with their mother's tears.

Then is this a fair life for everyone? Does the unfairness have a purpose? Could it teach us about what is right and what is not? Perhaps "number four" on the list should be "**to learn what is right and what is wrong**." Then we can continue our lives by those standards.

On the path of learning, we will have countless opportunities. We will be given as many chances to learn as there are raindrops. We will feel some of the raindrops, while some will fall next to us without touching us. We will learn the difference between right and wrong as we learn the difference between the dark and the light. However, learning will not complete your education for becoming wise. If you don't do anything with what you learn, you still need to think about the purpose of your education . That question alone will take you back to square one.

Why are we here?

So, shall we say number five on our list is "**put what you have learned into action**"? This gets interesting because humans will split at this level. Those who learned about right and wrong will get to choose if they want to practice right or wrong. The split creates two separate branches, and from those branches more branches split off. Because of the choices people make, some will spiral up, while some will spiral down.

Once again, we back to the topic of choices. There will be consequences to the choices you make. Your choice is not compelling until it is activated. Even then, the cycle is not complete because it needs to be fueled with your intention. So, number six on the list is "**choose between right and wrong.**"

Here is number seven: "**your intention will be the deciding factor in the outcome of your actions.**" Even when you want to do someone a favor, it still would not count as a favor, if your heart's intention is not in the right place. It is like volunteering for a good cause in order to build a more impressive résumé: it will not score well. If you actually want to hurt someone, and if that is your real intention, then the outcome of your action will not be good, either. Just as you can choose what you want to do, so you can also choose your intention.

Number eight is "**take responsibility for your actions.**" When you do that, you create an opportunity to redeem yourself. This is a great way to start waking up. Even if you made a choice while unconscious, you still have a chance to learn from it. You can still redeem yourself.

Taking responsibility for your actions does not only mean raising your hand to say, "Yes, I did it!". Because, after that statement, you need to do number nine on our list: "**facing the consequences.**" You will eventually have to face it. The choices and decisions you make and the actions you take come with consequences.

❖ Our choices define us.
❖ Our actions reinforce our choices.
❖ Our intentions fuel our actions.

Step number nine will test your ability. You can choose to stay strong and thrive in life, or you can choose to give up. Manifesting a mistake may take a minute, but paying for that mistake can take a lot longer. Some mistakes will cost you so much, you may end up losing your soul, your freedom, or even your life. This is the step where suffering becomes noticeable. This is when we might be finally paying attention. This is when number ten goes on the list: "**suffering consciously or not, when dealing with consequences.**"

When you are not aware of what you are going through, nothing can help you. None of the previous steps, collectively, help you skip step number ten. It will not happen. When you are unconscious, you are traveling along the delusional streets in a state of somnambulism. Until you really are awake, you cannot see what is happening or where you are. You are sleeping through the entire experience, too lazy to take a shower and wake up. This leads to the next step on the list, number eleven: "**Being interested in or being forced to being awake.**"

Imagine you smell smoke while you are sleeping, but you don't wake up because you are tired. Then your bed catches on fire. Would you wake up?

Most of us are not even aware of what we are really doing. Living like robots, we are only completing missions, finishing tasks or homework, and living because we are alive. Being alive doesn't mean we are awake. Going through life's journey does not offer us wisdom instantly.

So there has to be something more meaningful about being alive. Maybe there is a reason for us to be here, as humans. When your eyes are closed, you may try to see what is in front of you by using your mind's imagining ability. However, do not forget the mischievousness of the mind. Using your wild imagination, you can choose to imagine anything in any way that your mind can make happen for you.

Whether you voluntarily wake up or you are forced to wake up, you should take that as a blessing. Once you are awake, you will start to put together the pieces so your reason for learning through suffering starts to make more sense.

The next step is number twelve, where you have a great chance to understand more about your existence on this planet. "**Gaining wisdom.**"

Wisdom is your key to enlightenment. Wisdom may seem to take its time to visit us not because it plays with us, but because human beings are slow to get it. It is available for everyone.

Now, take a look at all the steps mentioned earlier:

1) Be alive.
2) Have the best version of your life.
3) Do not cling to your identity.
4) Learn what is right and what is wrong.
5) Put what you have learned into action
6) Choose between the right and the wrong.
7) Set your intention.
8) Take responsibility for your action.
9) Face the consequences.
10) Suffer consciously.
11) Wake up.
12) Gain wisdom.

Once you study these with full commitment, you may realize that life is energy, just like us. This energetic being called *life* gets shaped by us. It becomes whatever we want it to be. Your frequency will mold your contributions into life's production of its gift. So life basically will gift you back what you give to it. The percentage you invest in life will come back to you.

So, why are we here? Everybody has their version of an explanation at the level they are comfortable with, but, just for now, forget about any other possibilities. Forget about the creator, heaven or hell, aliens, vampires, witches, sirens, superheroes, werewolves, multiple dimensions, etc. Just for a minute, imagine we have no access to the collection of previous life data. That is inevitable, right? All you truly have is now. So, what do you want to do with your life? You don't know when it will end. What will you do with whatever time you have? Will you let it go to waste?

Think about your own reasons for being here, not the reasons for the entire human race. Only yours. That is how it starts. It all starts with you. You are here because you have a contribution to make. Your stories will be told and shared.

Remember, you only need to be in the here and now. Not in the past. Not in the future. You are here to take care of yourself, but not at the expense of others. You are here to care and share love, kindness, and compassion. You are here to create a beautiful art piece out of your life. You are here to set an example. You are here to wake up. You are here to claim your gift. Open it gently, handle it gently, show and share it gently, and pass its beauty along smoothly.

Be gentle, be kind, be loving, be compassionate, be caring, be awake, be emotional, be logical, be a dreamer, be an explorer, be an artist, be a scientist, be someone who spreads love, be a light-worker, and simply just be in the process of becoming your true self. Speak only the truth and be true. Free your true self. Allow whatever wants desperately to be released out of your existence. Do not waste this gift called life. Wake up! Your life is happening now.

37

CONFUSED STATE OF BEING

WHEN WE FALL, most of us don't feel the effects of hitting bottom right away. We don't notice the bruises ignited by the state of shock. We don't look up and try to calculate the height of the fall we have taken. We look down instead, as we lie flat on our face. Feeling the heaviness of our humility pressing down on our spine, we struggle to get up, hoping the muddy ground will hide us and that, perhaps, we can stay there until nobody remembers our awkward fall. In our graceless, broken body, we do not see any beauty in our human experiences.

Our eyes yearn to meet those who once witnessed our lives. We eventually learn to look in other directions for fear of witnessing their shame for us. Surrendering to loneliness starts to comfort our thoughts, as we survive in our confused state of being.

Lying on the ground with a little life to breathe, we may consider the option of giving up. We may even question our reasons for being alive. When all you see is the hopelessness of your reality, you may never want to hear your heart sing. You start covering your senses with mud, which already covers your skin.

Life seems like it has taken its own path without you in it. You cannot chase after it, nor can you ask it to wait for you. You start to assume that your legs have turned into mud and your sadness is starting to bury you in it. Being paralyzed dims the lights of your faith in your future, and you start to sink in. Then it starts to rain, as your fears turn into a flood. While you feel drenched in your own drama, the purity of the water coming from above falls on you persistently, as if it wants you to look up at. With the damaged and unused muscles of your neck, you lift your head up and ask why with your gloomy eyes.

Why did you fall from grace? Did someone push you? Did you lose your balance while you were so carefully walking the tightrope of your dull life? Did you arrange your own fall? If you did, why didn't you stage a more graceful fall?

You wait impatiently for the answer to that question. Your rage wants to prove you right about losing your faith. Your mind will conduct the symphony of crows in the dark, while you play the sad music of your heart. **When all you want to hear is the sound of your own music written by your disappointments, you will not listen to the music of other survivors**. Those who fell before you and decided to stand up have written their own music, too.

Your answer, however, might not be given to you in the form your heart desires. In fact, it could be delivered to you in such way that you have to decode it first. If you want an answer, you need to be able to listen for it. You need to turn the volume way down on your assumptions and on the voice of the victim inside you, who likely has been desperate the run the show.

For the most part, the answer you are looking for lies in the mud you have fallen in, but it is not easily noticeable, not like the sun above. You need to work for it; you need to use your senses and accept the fact that your ground is muddy.

One of the things that might slow down your ability to get answers is your mental state of being. Your confusion can extend the length of your awakening. You may even try to fall back asleep again. Once you are committed to finding your answers, you may notice the journey that lies ahead of you is full of aches and sorrow. But it is also filled with the joy of possibility to find an answer by discovering your truth.

While you lie on the ground after your fall, the first thing you need to do again is breathe.

Do not be afraid when you look at the pieces of your broken existence. It may seem impossible to put it back together, at first. Even if you did, you might be worried it would never look the same. You would always notice the glue patching it back together. Every time people look at you, they would see only your bruises and the visible lines of the patchwork.You would still wear your shame on the sleeves of your hand-me-down gown of humility. You think your broken life will eventually become the laughter of the Milky Way and every being on this planet will be able to see you. You may think you won't be revealed in darkness, but the darkness cannot cover the light entirely.

Your answer lies in the stitches of your patchwork. Every stitch represents a tear and your endurance. Your determination to live makes the thread so strong, you could capture any shark that dares to swim in the ocean of your confidence again. That thread does not have to be invisible. Your story will be read at the seams of your bodywork. **Being able to put yourself back together is one of the most admirable qualities that humans have**.

So, when your time comes to share your stories; when others want to know about those deep scars and stitch marks, tell them proudly why you decided to stand up after you fell. When you see another person with their own broken pieces and they do not know what to do, you can show them your scars.

Being broken into pieces is your opportunity to take a look at those pieces and be brave. Do not get discouraged, because, when you are broken, you may become the ringmaster of the circus of piteous beings. Those around you who judge you too quickly and thoughtlessly may never be courageous enough to look at their own wounds.

Nevertheless, some of us fall into our feathered beds, and some of us fall into the minefields. The harder the fall, the greater the opportunity to learn. **The more fearful we are, the darker becomes what we see.**

Have you ever been presented with such opportunity?

38

THE CIRCUS OF THE PITEOUS BEINGS

MOST OF US, at some point in our lives, have been part of a circus of the piteous beings, either as a spectator or a performer. Regardless our position, we all breathe the same air in that circus. But some of us inhale humility and exhale shame beneath our costumes. Where we perform the act of a happy clown, under our makeup we wear the sad face of an ignored ghost. Simultaneously, we inhale ignorance and exhale carelessness under the rock where we hide.

When the show turns sideways, when the clowns throw away their costumes and the tiny creatures face the sun, our broken pieces start to recognize each other. In each broken piece is an answer waiting to be found. You start to lay everything on the table of your honesty. You are no longer ashamed of your bruises. You no longer feel you need to cover yourself and hide your nakedness. You start to focus on one task: putting yourself back together.

Your soul's energy looks around patiently until it recognizes something very familiar. Behind the tall trees and under the muddy lakes, far from the warmth of the home and next to the frozen roses, under the concrete coldness of forgotten love stories and the untold version of your suffering, the music of your heart decides to play again. Your soul's energy fetches the music of your heart first, then brings it to the spot where you lie only half hopeful.

The tiny pieces recognize the music, which once played so loudly. This same music brings the pieces together. After spending many hopeless and sorrowful nights under the stars, where you shared your sadness with trees, and at the bottom of the oceans, where you had to toss your dreams away, and underneath the ground, where you have been buried, your heart becomes the first part to be pieced together completely, albeit with stitches and bruises.

Your soul's energy whispers to your heart, "Sing with all you have, and let them come to you."

The melody rises above the obstacles. The sounds of sorrow and pain switch places with hope and joy. The song you sing lifts you up and it becomes easier to see your entire broken self. You cherish every part of you with compassion and without any judgment. You rise above your once demolished existence and allow your identity to turn into dust.

Knowing the self is everywhere, you start to collect your pieces. Despite all the challenges and being lost in your own life, you no longer preach to the choir. Your music makes your painful journey bearable. In the neverending yearning for your loved ones, you keep writing your music, believing they will someday hear it, no matter how far away they are.

This is how love keeps our broken heart warm and intact. In the circus of life, when we perform in front of others, we sometimes forget about ourselves, hidden underneath all the costumes and makeup. But every show comes to an end. The performer goes back to his chair in front of the mirror in his dressing room. He starts to clean his face slowly, while entertaining many thoughts in his mind. His hands reveal the wrinkles on his face as they take the blues off his skin. Some of the lines on his face remind him of good times, as he looks at his reflection, but some do not. The man in the mirror looks back at him as if he wants him to know he'll always be there.

Wounded souls, broken hearts, and damaged hopes can survive when they seek the light. They can look at their reflection in muddy waters and still recognize their inner light.

In this circus, however, it is not easy to witness everyone's laughter when your heart continues to cry. When the show is over and we start to walk toward home, sometimes we take a path with no street lights. The darkness breathes on our neck while our steps become shakier. We keep hearing about the inner child, but sometimes it is hard to face the child we have left behind.

Every time we perform, we put on a mask. We get used to receiving attention. It feels more alive to perform when we know our soul is dying inside. The revival of forgotten joy requires commitment, even when you feel like you were left behind. It takes courage to claim your life back when all you see is its remnants.

How about the ones who are there to watch the show of your coming undone? Would they ever be interested in seeing the real faces of the performers? Would they recognize anything familiar? Do we see ourselves in others' show of survival?

If you stop your performance, other people may not be happy with your decision. Any unexpected happening can create discomfort, especially for the ones who have become accustomed to seeing you the certain way. Their routine comfort in familiarity is their way of accepting you and how you have been performing.

However, some of us wake up from our coma unexpectedly. All of a sudden, our paralyzed legs start to move, and our hearts start to beat again. When we stand in front of the usual audience, we bare our soul without any fear of being rejected because, at that point, our truth overcomes any spectator's criticism or expectation. At that point, our new journey to freedom has already begun.

What a circus this life is.

39

CONSTRUCTING YOUR WINGS

SOMETIMES, WE FORGET what we are made of. We look at the broken part of a human soul and get discouraged. We witness so many fallen trees, so many broken bridges, so many cemeteries—so much of every form of suffering. Because of our fear of the unknown, we get comfortable living life within the boundaries of our cowardice and do not often step outside the walls of our insecurity.

But how far can we go in this life, if we never leave the comfort zone of our backyard? How can we truly know how the ground feels if we never fall down? How can we know what it's like to see from above if we never leave the ground?

Those who burn with the fire of being bored with their lives should consider coming out of their houses painted with the colors of their own drama. Humans have a tendency to get comfortable with their own routine life, so they do not seek paths to explore. Those who mistakenly believe they can see everything from their chair in front of the television complete their life's journey without desiring to construct their wings, because anyone who has only seen what was in front of them can't ever realize that, on their back, they indeed have wings.

When you are curious about a color you have imagined but never seen, start to create that color by mixing the colors you already have. You might not ever discover what you have but didn't think you had, if you are afraid to live your life fully. You will not find your truth, if you are a slave to your identity.

When you get a moment, take a look at those who have achieved what was once believed unimaginable. How did they do it? Some were told they could never walk again, but they did. What inspired humans to create planes? Birds, perhaps? Why did we visit the moon? Someday, the cure for cancer will reveal itself to us. It is not about who is going to find the cure. The cure is already here. And it will reveal itself.

In this world, a great deal of energy exchange has been happening. The tension is tight between the good and the bad, the positive and the negative, and the darkness and the light. **The cure for any disease resides in the untouchable places between opposites**. And those people who figure out such cures, solutions, and answers have the curiosity to see what else might be out there.

Sometimes, when we go hiking, we get lost and end up taking an unfamiliar path, only to realize later that there was a reason for that. Do you know when we figure those things out? When we are not clinging to the result and so are least expecting it. Right? When we are in those untouchable places between the opposites.

So, where do you think you can find your true self? Between the darkness and the light? Between the good and the bad? When you are right in the middle of opposites, your body receives powerful energy from both sides that forces you to come out of your shell, your identity. It shocks you so strongly, it dumps out all the data on your self-centeredness, so you may feel empty and naked.

But if it weren't for the dire straits of life, how would you ever get the opportunity to gain wisdom? And if it weren't for suffering, how would you know what you are made of?

Do not take your breath for granted. Your life's energy travels between the rhythms of your heartbeat and your breath. And those two can stop instantly.

Ask yourself, "Am I really what I think and what I see I am?" Are you?

You are more than what you think you see in the mirror. **You have the ability to adjust and mold yourself into anything, when you know your life depends on it.** So, get out of your comfort zone. Turn your television off. Start visualizing your wings. You may be doing just fine without them. But, someday, if you find yourself at the bottom of the sea, you will have to turn into a creature of the sea to survive, and the sea may not allow you to swim back to shore as your old self.

Your wings are the bridges that your train of hopes will travel on; never underestimate their value. Your freedom will never be true if you fail to leave your chamber of doubt. **If we are interested in reaching our destination, we should also learn to go with the flow when presented with a new route.**

But if fear is the fuel that keeps our lives going, are we really free? Can your wings help you rise above the fear? When you live in a world of suffering, you may see the sky differently. It could become separated from the ground that seems to be swallowing you and the transparent membranes of your reality that keep you in. You may get confused. It is like having but not holding. It is like seeing a flower but not being able to smell it.

It is all internal. When you lose your faith in yourself, your life meets you half way. The shoulders that carry us to the sea of life cannot be so doubtful. Otherwise, just like a dam with a small crack, the pressure of the water will destroy whatever is holding you together and helping you keep going in life.

If others tell you they cannot see the wings on your back, you might feel discouraged or disappointed. But if you do not believe you have wings, that might actually destroy the bridges. The trains of your hopes may never come to get you at the station of your sorrows. Do not doubt your ability to rise above whatever might be holding you back.

We seem to be paying quite a bit attention to what others think of us. Unfortunately, every time we fall for that, we take a step back. This "two steps farther, one step back" attitude can actually suck the joy out of our journey to self-discovery. We may feel like abandoning everything. The option to give up might start to flirt with your deceived heart.

Consider again before you give up. Try to remember the victories of those who claimed their wings. Life can be very challenging at times; it can really come after your soul and may not treat you fairly. But then, sometimes, that is exactly what we need. **Sometimes a kick in the rear, a slap on the face, and the truth nailed on our forehead can wake us up faster than a pat on the shoulder.**

Do not throw away the lessons gifted to you by both the darkness and the light. You will realize that the suffering, which may feel really dark, is actually also sponsored by the light. Do not just skip through your life. It is okay to stop to dance in the rain and get soaked in your most fancy outfit.

Never wait to tell someone you love them until the perfect moment within your own reality. Go ahead and become your own best friend. When you send love and light to the universe, do not forget you are also a part of it. If you accept you can fall from above, remember you can also get up.

40

EPHEMERAL ENVY

ENVY DOES EXIST and it can visit anyone during their lifetime. Unfortunately, it can become a permanent resident within some of us. It can come into our bed and sleep next to our loneliness and greed.

However, just like any other thought or feeling, envy is not meant to be permanent. These feelings are ships passing through our life. They are the seasons not meant to last forever. Thoughts and feelings are meant to be channeled. We do not have to assume ownership of them. Instead, we should try to see them as part of a transformation designed for all of us to experience. Unfortunately, unlike the butterfly's, our transformation can take longer and can come with a price tag, too.

Can covetousness be channeled? If it can, do we get to choose what to do with that feeling? Or should only a certain outcome be expected from channeling envy? Does envy even have a purpose? If you hold onto it for too long, will it burn you or anyone or anything around you?

Envy has a purpose. But its purpose will not be revealed to you until you suffer its consequences. And it will not only burn you; it will burn whatever or whomever you might have around you. Some of us will be able to see the remnants of its purpose in the cooled-down ashes of our regrets. While you may think the empty victory of envy cools you like snowflakes in summer, on the contrary, it dips you in the boiling-hot water of the witch's brew. When you are exposed to extreme cold or hot, can you think clearly? If you cannot think clearly, you are diverted by uninvited thoughts. When you don't notice you have once again left the door of your unmindfulness wide open, it can be difficult for you to take responsibility for your carelessness, because you are not aware.

For you to comprehend the moral of a story, you need to be mindful. **Just like it is difficult to see a fish in cloudy water, you have no clarity when your mind is muddy.**

Envy, like any other damaging emotion, pushes you to experience falling into a downward spiral. What is the purpose of falling into a downward spiral? Do we really have to learn our lessons the hard way all the time? Not really. But, when an experience is hard, it becomes more difficult to forget. Something that causes too much suffering can leave a deeper scar, and some scars become so deeply embedded that nothing seems to be magical or supernatural enough to remove their origin from our memory. Even if the mind overlooks it, your body and soul will remember it.

Once you experience the aftershock of acting under the influence of envy, you will realize the damage it causes almost immediately, provided you are willing to see this. Otherwise, you'll continue your sleepwalking, and envy will extend its stay in your home. Then, your envy will turn into a morning glory that starts to take over, climbing over all the plants, trees, bushes, and flowers in your garden. Can you stop it from consuming everything you have?

Envy is there for a reason, but this emotion is a force to be reckoned with. It will not leave until you are ready. If you are interested in being healthy and having a peaceful life, you better let go of the envy in your heart. It is very poisonous, and while it tries to bite others, it bites you, too. Regardless how you try to avoid it, it will leave bite marks on you.

Think about what you are envious of. Who do you think is holding onto envy? The answer once again is "your child-self." If envy is running the show, there is no easy way to hide or deny it. It is too strong to miss. You need to have a sincere chat with yourself, because it is going to come down to one thing:

"They have what I want... How come I don't have it?"

That is the foundation, the roots of your tree, consumed by ill-will combined with jealousy. Hopefully, you will realize that whatever you want but don't have can actually be invited into your life, too. The only person standing in the way of your having what you want is *you*. However, instead of focusing on whatever it is that you think you absolutely must have, at least consider another approach. Look at it from another perspective. Do you really *have* to have it? Or are you jealous because someone else has it instead of you? How would your life look if you knew you would *never* have it?

Chasing after material things or after fame and superiority is like chasing your own shadow. As long as you have envy and continue to feed it, you will never be satisfied with what you already have. While you are riding your Pegasus, you will complain about not having a griffin. Nothing will be enough for you.

There is actually something more seriously damaging about envy, and that is not going after what you want, but instead going after the person who has what you want.

We sometimes make poor decisions and, as a result, find ourselves in situations we could never have imagined in our wildest dreams. Sooner or later, your envy will take you to a place where the darkness is your only house for seeking refuge in. How are you going to find your way back home?

Let's make this a bit simpler. One thing can defeat envy. It is called "being grateful." When you feel truly blessed and thankful for what you have, the cells in your body discharge envy. Every time you get caught in the iron net of envy, try to see whether you can be thankful for what you already have. If you cause someone's life to be altered by your envy—if someone loses their job, relationship, or credibility—please know that redeeming yourself will not be easy. Never destroy a life. Never kill someone's hopes and dreams. Never steal someone's life. Your envy already steals from your own life.

41

STOIC HUGS

YOUR COMMITMENT level defines what your product will look like. There is a magical contract between a life and who is in it. Life is willing to give you what you want to the same degree of your commitment to getting what you want.

If you want to learn a different language, you need to study it. If you want to be good at whatever you want to do, you have to practice and you have to focus. How about love? Is this true for love, as well? If you want to have love, how does life reply to your request? If there is so much loneliness and untouched hearts in this world, does it mean we do not know how to give and receive love?

Love can be both conditional and unconditional. Love also can be a great tool to get what you want. Love, however, is easy to recognize. When there is love, life looks and feels different. When your love is conditional, its sincerity is questionable. And the person for whom your love is intended will get your love, but her heart will remain unignited. When you share your love, be genuine and sincere. Even the statue you carved out of marble will be able to feel your love if it is for real. So many exchanges take place between beings. How do we know, then, what is real and what is not?

True love is always unconditional. It is humans who label it and put a price on it. You are the conduit. **Love is universal**, and every being carries a piece of it. How could you think that love won't find its other piece? Love always finds a way to come to you.

When you are stoic,what do you think you are contributing to your environment? Isn't your state of indifference adding more gray to your life? When you live life as a stoic, what do you think you will get from life, in return? Are stoics sleepwalkers? Love, however, has the ability to generate enough energy to reshape your thought process. As human beings, we are meant to experience love.

Anything given conditionally cannot possibly come from a place where nothing is expected in return. When you expect, you get attached. Whatever you give should originate from the sincerity of your existence. And the love you have grows bigger when it is shared.

Think about the bargains you have made with life. Remember those trades? Well, here is some information about the deals we make with life. Whether consciously or not, you made an agreement with life. You said, "When I grow up, I want to become this or that." "When I am twenty-eight, I want to become wealthy." "When I retire, I want to do this or that." And, of course, so many other statements, wish lists, desires, commitments, and more. Right?

Well, who do you think has access to the wish lists of all living beings?

Your requests get delivered through a line that has two receivers. On the one hand, the coordinator of the light takes your orders. How about the other end of the receiver? Yes, the coordinator who works for the darkness. Predictable, right?

When you make your wish about becoming wealthy when you turn twenty-eight, it receives a lot of attention. Your wish gets sent to the producers' office. They discuss all the scenarios. Screenwriters show up, and all the scenarios get embellished. The same process takes place at headquarters for both sides. Two opposites are at work: the light and the darkness. They both are focused and determined to see your wish come true.

So, the results come in. Your request gets approved. All the scenarios are tested, and the possibility of your wish becoming a reality is very likely.

You become wealthy at the age of twenty-eight. How does it feel? Do you feel like you just hugged yourself, congratulating your success, but somehow you feel emotionless? Or are you crying because you actually made it happen? At what price? Do you know who sponsored you? Do you know who funded your project? Was it the light or the darkness?

When we want something, we mail our request to the universe. But we seem to forget to address our envelope properly. Poorly addressed letters go to the department of oblivion, located at the corner of a black hole, in the building of "up for grabs."

Some mail is specifically titled "the ghost of the darkness," "my grandmother's spirit," "the fairies of the enchanted lands," and go ahead, pick your own.

So, even though you get what you wanted, you still don't seem happy. Why is that?

Is the chocolate cake you asked for now in front of you, but you cannot taste the chocolate? Is there a feeling of uneasiness in your gut? Does it feel like the victory you had won is not fair?

No matter how brilliantly we act, deep down inside we know how it feels. We know if we are true or not. We know if we are giving our love conditionally or not. We know if we indeed earned that medal rightfully or not.

When you want something before it gets addressed to the universe, take a look around you first. Do you have room for it? Will it go well with everything else you have? What is the price tag? Do you really need it? Do you want it for yourself? Or are you trying to compete with your neighbors? Your request will be answered, so you better be ready when it comes and knocks on your door.

Perhaps this is why we should take responsibility for the suffering we experience. We are actually the initiators of the whole thing. Even if the request we sent was ten years ago does not mean it had to be answered right then.

In our confused state, we ask why is this happening to us now. You believe you did not do anything to deserve this suffering, so why now? What did you do to deserve it? Maybe nothing you can recall right away. But if you dig into it, you may realize how it all started.

Think before you ask. Address your envelope correctly and apply the proper postage before you mail it. Your mail will go to the point of no return and your request will be answered, but not when it is most convenient for you.

And if you think the darkness is the only side pushing you into suffering, you are incorrect. The darkness may lure you in, but, actually, the light may present that opportunity to you because, if the light has given up on you, you will never wake up from your sleep. **Given your suffering, you will have the opportunity to wake up at your own pace.**

For all the encounters you have had, try to remember in what percentage you were actually your true self. For all the pretending you did, for all the masks you wore and all the trades in which you sold a piece of your heart, for all the cold hugs you gave, choices you made against your heart, and lies you told to yourself and others, try to remember who has been the catalyst of this suffering gifted to you by the light.

If the light gave up on you, would it allow you to skip through the daisies all the time, every day of your life?

How else will you wake up, if suffering does not shake your ground?

Remember that your love is unconditional. You are free to share your life, but there is one crucial step. **Your love will never be enough for anyone if they have not learned to love themselves first**. The same goes for you, too. When you feel unloved, the door to your heart has a sign on it that you don't see. It reads:

Closed for business.

The owner has lost the keys to his own shop.

Start with yourself. If love is missing in your life because you still have not found the courage to look within first, you need to learn to embrace the being you were born with. Love for yourself *does* need to get activated first. Love is magnetic. If you want to

receive it from others, you need to start loving yourself first.
Do not ignore your suffering. When your love for yourself is
activated, the light will start to find its way in the darkened veins of
your heart. Your blood will gladly carry reminders of the beautiful
things about yourself and all the good things you have done during
your lifetime. Then you will know how to address your label. It will
say:

> The Department of Awakening—The Division of being True
> to Self.

The next time you hug, do not hide your love. **If you truly love
someone, make sure they know it, even if you fail to tell them.**
Love always finds its way back to those who love themselves.

42

ON THE BRIDGE OF CHOICES

YOU WILL BE given many opportunities in your life time to make choices. Some of those choices will put you right in the middle of exact opposites. Some of you will be paralyzed with fear that you are making a wrong decision. It is like standing on a bridge and not being sure which way to go. If you choose to go left, you know a part of you will still be thinking about what would have happened if you chose to go right, instead. If you choose to go right, a part of you will be thinking about the left side of the bridge.

We have all been on this particular bridge. We all have lingered there, some of us longer than others. Some of us crossed that bridge with absolute certainty, some of us were forced to pass, some of us were sleeping while crossing, and some of us did not even care.

But how many of us took a deep breath and looked at the path where we came from while we stood on that bridge? How many of us really wondered what might be waiting for us on the other side of the bridge of choices? Did we see anyone or anything familiar on that bridge?

Did we walk there? Was our walk to the bridge filled with

struggles?

There is a time where we may find ouselves pausing before making a decision. The moment that the pause takes place is like building a bridge anchored by the surprises of the unknown and the mysteries of the unseen. It is always possible we do not understand the logic behind some of our choices. Sometimes, we make choices without thinking.

From a distance, we may become intrigued and develop a neverending curiosity about the other side of our reality. Sometimes, we get bored standing on the same old ground, and we yearn for something different. We long for a change and an opportunity that takes us away from the monotony of life. Lives spent under the sky where there was nothing to see push us onto the ships, regardless of our knowing where our journey may take us.

Some of us start such a journey by leaving our loved ones behind and covering our ears so we do not hear their cries. Although we know there is not enough distance between us, **sometimes we leave the ones we love on the shores of our longing and continue on our journey with broken hearts**.

When we are on that bridge, we may think there is only one ship waiting for us. Sometimes we get fascinated by the lights coming from other ships but never realize those lights are only temporary, staged by the darkness. We become attracted to those ships and leave our former life behind.

We really are not equipped with enough wisdom and experience to judge anyone making their choices on that bridge. Sooner or later, all of us will sit down and recall the journey of our soul while we were on that bridge, making our own choices.

This bridge is like a portal. When you make your choice, the portal is immediately connected to different portals. The choice you make creates endless possibilities for activating new beginnings and pausing old ones. Because nothing is permanent and everything changes in time, some of the paused memories can come back into your life. The choice you make can also separate you from your familiar, safe ground. You may find yourself smelling foreign flowers in the unfamiliar gardens of unknown territories.

Regardless of our being aware of the choices we make, there

are always underlying reasons behind our decisions. We may never be able to figure some of them out, but they do exist for those of us who are interested in bringing them to light.

When someone finds himself on that bridge, it does not mean they knew how they got there. Some people sleepwalk, some become intoxicated, some are lured into it, and some simply follow the fumes of their burnt hopes or the scent of their lust's perfume. We all visit that bridge.

However, some of us never come back from their journey. They jump off the bridge and land on a very specific ship. No one knows where that ship's port is. Before they actually jump off, they might have an idea of the destination but not the location of the actual port. When they jump off, choosing their destiny, the ones left behind never give up kneading the rope made of their tears, hoping to get them back. But those who jumped off don't come back in their body. The sun continues to rise, but they never feel its warmth. The stars shine brightly, but they never notice their light. They start to melt in their version of suffering, looking out to sea with hopes that another ship will come back from the port where their loved one have gone. Time goes by as they learn to survive, but their hearts never learn to fill their emptiness.

Some seats can never be filled. Even then, we should not judge those who chose to travel to ports that require only a one-way ticket.

Some of us choose a different ship, one that accommodates those with mistakes and stupidity. Everyone on board gets a chance to compare their foolishness. Some realize quicker than most that their ship's journey will be on disturbed seas. The waves will be high enough to feed their fear, but not higher than their shame or guilt. Those people will eventually know that if they want to come back, they have to obey the rules of either one of the ship's captains. One of the captains is carved out of stone and reinforced with steel; he is colder than ice and poisonous, so stern as to destroy any form of sympathy. When you see this captain and he talks to you, he reminds you of the consequences of your choice.

The other captain is carved out of the trunk of the giving tree. He still allows everyone, regardless their mistakes, to get some rest as he cradles them with his branches. The captain keeps all the love letters that have ever been written to you, every laughter-filled memory, every hope that lights your eyes, and every reason for you to go back. When you are ready, you go back to the shores you came from holding your head high and keeping your heart open for love, kindness, and compassion.

On this journey, you will be visited mostly by the serpents of the sea, but the dolphins will find a way to cheer you. You will be primarily served your own tears, but your body will learn to quench its thirst with them. You will learn to recycle your aches and you will re-use your regret, but you will learn never to throw away your lesson.

Unfortunately, not everyone will learn on this ship. Everyone will be tested; temptations will be served by sirens, recognitions will be announced by mermaids, the ghosts of the pirates will try to trick you by promising you the treasures of the kings of their imagination, and both captains will be there to answer you.

Those who pass will never be the same. Their soul will come back not with shame, but with light. Their hearts will touch others not with rage, but with compassion. They will share their story not with pride, but with humility.

Those who do not pass will continue their life's journey on a different ship. As long as they are alive, they will always have an opportunity for redemption and healing.

The ones who come back with wisdom will become light-workers. They will live among us who are always exposed to the darkness and the light. They will never judge anyone, and they will not give up on you.

There will be so many more ships that will take people from one port to another. Those of us who think we will never leave the shore are incorrect. You cannot truly believe the shore you stand on is real. It is only the product of your conniving mind.

43

MASQUERADE OF MORTALS

THIS IS A PLACE where everyone is invited. We all get to dress up any way we want and we are free to choose a mask to cover our faces. Although invited, not everyone participates in these masquerades, which are held in every house, every street, every neighborhood of each city everywhere in our world. Anyone can choose to join any one of these balls and wear all types of masks.

Why do we wear a mask? Are we afraid to be recognized? Do we want to reveal ourselves when the time is right and only to the special ones in our lives? **Do we enjoy seeing others wondering about who we really are under the mask we wear?**

It is a good feeling to know we can indeed step out of our daily clothes and dress up as anything we want. Like someone who is doing the same thing all day then decides to do something else for once in his lifetime. Or someone who wears the same uniform all the time now wants to wear something different for a change.

Some of the clothes we wear are special and available only to certain people. They may come with the condition we sign a contract in order to have access to them. Who is the tailor behind these fancy outfits? Who is the designer of your masquerade? The sad thing is that some of us live in constant masquerades and assume we will be charged for their expense. Yes, there is a bill associated with it, and you will pay it.

Let's go back to a time when you wanted desperately to step out of your daily life because it felt boring, and you wanted to experience something different. You probably knew that what you wanted to try could possibly come back and bite you. After all, perhaps you had seen your friends do it, and so you wanted to give it a try.

Your friends provided you the information about a specific masquerade. However, you were worried because you did not have a costume and mask to wear. You could not go there wearing usual clothes and a face that can easily be recognized by everyone who has seen you before. So your friend took you to a dressmaker who had many masks for every personality and mistake. You picked a costume and a mask. You felt unstoppable. Before you left the dressmaker's shop, he reminded you of the contract you had to sign. You hesitated at first, but ended up signing it anyway. After all, you figured you could not be the only one who'd been in that situation before.

While at the party, you felt like you could conquer anything. Your friends told you to keep the costume and mask as long as you wanted. You were empowered by your new customized look.

You got used to dressing differently until, one day, your heart became allergic to what you were wearing. You chose to ignore it at first, but your body did not surrender. Your body wanted you to pay attention.

You decided to take the costume and mask back to the dressmaker. However, when you got there, you couldn't find his shop. You did not realize that the night you visited him with your friends, you were actually sleepwalking and did not really know where you were. You got scared and started to panic. You didn't know who to tell what you thought was happening.

You ran to your friend's house in despair. With tears in her eyes, his mom told you about a ship that her son was on. She said that ship was about to leave shore. You started to run downhill, hoping to ask him how he managed to get away. By the time you finally arrived at the shore, your friend's special ship with two captains was already on its way to a very special cruise on disturbed seas.

Your head dropped down, and your heart felt heavy. You had long ago forgotten about your broken wings and felt as if your blood was muddy. You noticed a figure like a statue. Apparently, he was waiting for you without moving. Once you were ready to pass him by, he called your name, catching you by surprise. He told you about your story and the tailor of your masquerade. How could he possibly know all about this, you wondered, sure that the guilt you had been carrying had never been shared with anyone else? How could he know you so well?

He looked at you and said: "If you want, you can get on that ship, but not tonight, because you need to be on the bridge of choices first. That is where you will choose your own ship. Because of the regret in your heart, the right ship will pick you up. That is all I can tell you."

Then, just like the tailor earlier, he, too, disappeared. You looked up where he pointed, in the direction of the bridge of choices, and, in your own confusions, being stuck between hope and anxiety, you took your first step on the bridge. You saw many others there, some still wearing their costumes and some holding their masks between broken fingers, lingering and yet not knowing how and what to choose.

The tailor, who was also the mask maker, went back to his headquarters, where he worked as a recruiter for the human resources of the darkness.

The other person who knew your story and guided you to the bridge of choices also went back to his headquarters, where he worked a recruiter for the human resources of the light.

While you were on the bridge, you thought of your friend and looked at the other people on the bridge. You wondered if you would make the right decision. Then you began to worry what would happen if the tailor brought you another costume. Would you be strong enough to say no? Would your heart surrender to the dressmaker's mask? Would someone prevent you from falling again? Would this ship of yours bring you back? Or would you be left behind in your isolation?

As you started to think about your life, you didn't notice the time as it stopped. You thought you were now paralyzed, but everyone else was moving. Your life felt like it had lost its meaning because of what you signed with the tailor. Before you lost hope entirely, you noticed some of the others on the bridge lining up to board a ship. You asked them quietly, and one of them showed you his one-way ticket. You didn't understand why anyone would purchase a one-way ticket. Would they not want to come back?

You started to consider the same option, entertaining the idea of not coming back. Wouldn't life continue without you? Would your decision be considered selfish?

Your suffering started only because of your heart's allergic reaction to the costume and mask you were wearing. If your life was not worth it and if you did not have any more reasons to continue, why did your heart try to wake you up? In the middle of your drowning, if the dolphins came and saved you, would that not be a reason for you to wake up? **Your suffering started because you were not yet done with life**. But you were too green and fresh to understand the value of suffering on your first night. First, you drank your own remedy, and it tasted bitter. On the bridge of choices, you noticed the ship boarding all those holding one-way tickets. You looked at the gap between them and your feet. Your mind might have encouraged you to go to that line and join them, if you were ready. However, if it is not your time yet, your heart will not let you go.

44

THIRST

THIRST IS THE REASON for your suffering. Feel free to pick your own reason, if you want. However, the thing that ignites the fire is your thirst.

Thirst runs in your bloodstream like a racehorse running in the wild. Thirst is your desire. No matter what angle you choose to look at it from, either positive or negative, your desire will cause suffering because, sooner or later, it will turn into a clinging. You will become attached to whatever your senses cling to. Once you are attached, you are hooked.

You will try to find a way to quench your thirst until it manifests and you get what you desire. But during this journey, you will be overtaken by the intensity of your desire and will become a slave to your thirst.

Desire comes with duality. You could be thirsty for love or vengeance. You could be thirsty to construct or destroy. You could be thirsty for anything in your mortal life. You may be committed to completing your bucket list before your life ends. You may not realize that desire can control your actions and may find yourself in a place where you would plant the seeds of your suffering.

Thirst is the main ingredient in desire, greed, lust, craving, passion, rapture, ecstasy, obsession, rage, urge, hunger, and… you name it! **Whatever you crave will never lose its ability to flirt with you, if you are not controlled in your senses**. Your mind will not stop clinging onto whatever you want, and even if you do not want to admit it, you could become obsessed about it. It is like a fire: the flames will never go out because your clinging continues to add more wood to it.

You need to learn to see the need for craving for what it is, but not in the picture created through your mind's ability to betray. What you may not realize, due to lack of wisdom, is that, when you chase after your thirst, you no longer live freely in that moment because, in that precise moment, you are only consumed with one thing, which is getting what you want. All of your senses have already created an alliance. Desire burns you. Your passion dehydrates you. Your lust fills your veins with polluted air.

So you get on your horse and start the hunt. Be careful about what you want, what you choose to catch, because your choice, just like everything else, can come from either the darkness or the light. When you want something really badly, that "want" is actually "clinging." As long as you are clinging, your attachment creates your expectations. And your expectations are traps, setting you up. The only thing that can get caught is your disappointment.

Your disappointment paves the way to your suffering. Also, be careful about what you do not want. What "you don't want" is actually "clinging," as well. So your thirst lives in duality. Whether you want or you don't, you are hooked.

That is the foundation of heedlessness that will open a chapter in your life. This chapter will be called "suffering."

When you choose without awareness of actually choosing, your choice can contain any ingredient and could be a combination of both natural and artificial. You need to remember that even not choosing is indeed "choosing."

If you do not pay attention, you could become a target of solicitors who will not stop selling you something. The currency you use to purchase whatever you desire is nothing but your free will.

On the flip side, the resistance you build against whatever you do not want is also nothing but your free will, as well.

The energy you use to express whether your desire toward something is positive or your strong resistance is negative is actually the same. It may be confusing to visualize that we still use energy on something even if we *do not* want to have. We may think, if we know what we do not want, we really do not have to think about it anymore and, therefore, do not need to use any more of our energy on that, right?

Wrong!

Our machinelike programmed existence creates connections and assigns tasks. It keeps guard in front of your house to prevent intruders from entering. It is your energy that keeps those guards employed. It is just like hiring a personal shopper to get you whatever you desire. The energy of your existence that will still attach you to the darkness or the light. Only you can choose between the two.

However, there is also the third option. That is the *middle way*. This is a state of mind where you are no longer controlled by your likes or dislikes. This place is not a place of numbness or coma. On the contrary, this place is where you are more awake and mindful. You will realize that **a desire can be a poisonous water you drink to satisfy your thirst, especially when your mind figures out how to make you feel thirsty again**. Then you will soon find yourself chasing after a new way of satisfying your thirst. When your stubborn efforts figure out new ways to be satisfied, not only you will lose control of your wild animals, but those animals will capture anyone in their way in order to get what they want. This is the beginning of your addiction, as your craving and clinging will arrive shortly after that.

Clinging is not a baby who sleeps peacefully. It creates many sleepless nights for you. It will be hungry and never be satisfied. It will either be too cold or too hot. When what you have is not enough, desire becomes your bloodhound and chases anything, dead or alive.

Think about the middle way, where you are aware of both the negative and the positive. There, you can simply say, "The energy I have is supporting me to feel thankful for what I have."

45

TUNNELS OF DESPAIR

WHEN YOUR TEARS carry the sorrow of your heartache, they fall so heavily, it seems nothing can stand in their way. They turn into rivers whose current steals your hopes away, and in your blooming despair, you find yourself listening to sad songs.

All the laughter of the world stops speaking your language. At the darkest hours of the night, you start to dig tunnels to escape. Your fingers bleed against the harsh rejection of the earth. Nobody else can fit inside the tunnels of your inconsolable devastation. You continue to dig in the dark. When it gets cold at night, the wolves howl in your heart as you yearn for company.

Your tunnels, however, will never take you to the light. In your own confusion, you cannot realize that your tunnels are spiraling downward. Every exhale rips your hope right out of your chest. Your light seems to grow dimmer as you close your eyes to your reality. Life feels unfair in your bruised thoughts. The bats seem to purchase your sight, but you hardly care. When nothing is worth seeing, when no air is clean enough to breathe, when there is no hand close enough to hold, no shoulder available to lean on, and no hole small enough for you to avoid, you cannot stop falling into the dark suffering in your heart. **When your heart is in the custody of disappointments, you have a harder time breaking free from the prison of martyrdom**.

When you lose faith, you plant the seeds of isolation. When the seasons change, you reap only the moldy crop of your loneliness.

This is a mistake we make. We refuse the company of friends when we feel depressed. Whatever the remnants of our logic instruct, we surrender to it. It is as if we can no longer think about finding a solution, so we throw in the towel. Our senses lose their nutrients. We then close the doors and lock them from inside. Just like a child who is afraid to be visited by a monster, we live in fear of being visited by the fall of our straw empire. Perhaps we do not need help after all.

Here is another mistake we make: We think we do not need help. We all need it, and you need to get over this idea. Not everyone will know how to offer their help, just as not everyone feels comfortable receiving help.

As you head toward healing, you will visit many different places and people. You will also receive postcards from many people who live in many different places. Some of them will connect with you effortlessly, and some will stir the hornet's nest. Some people will put a Band-Aid on your wounds, while some people will not be able to look at the wound, and some may poke it with an ice pick. But **on your healing journey, you will be offered help from the light**. You will not be abandoned. When you find yourself in a place where assassinating your own life might look like a good idea, you should pinch or slap yourself so you can wake up.

46

INACCESSIBLE ROUTES

BECOMING IMMUNE to your defeats is a dead-end street. Your heart is on strike, your molecules are lost, your hopes have been kidnapped, and your faith is arrested. You cannot see the paths used by others who have discovered the truth about themselves. The child in your heart is not interested in playing outside. The sun no longer visits you.

You look around as if nothing you see is real. You start to believe that all routes are inaccessible.

Can one become immune to hopelessness? Can you go on, even if there is no ground? Can you survive each moment constantly filled with sorrow? Can you unlock the doors of your captivated state of mind?

Some paths are designed to ambush you. Some routes are not interconnected. **There are journeys from which you cannot return.** There are people out there who will tell you to go a certain direction only. Some will guide you in the opposite direction. You will come across some signs that mislead you and do not help you to resolve your puzzle. There will be lessons given to you in a language you do not comprehend. You will order opportunities, but they will be delivered to others instead, not to you. You will purchase an ounce of peace, but it will be quarantined at the border. Your ticket to sanity will expire. **Some bridges will take you nowhere**.

Why?

Isn't it already inconvenient to be falling down while everyone you know seems to be moving on? So what is the reason to have to face more hurdles? Are we being tested? Why? By who? Is it because we are here to witness the decaying of the soul in our lamentable existence? Are we set up to fail? If we pass, what for? What will we win?

Perhaps we accepted this challenge as we were being prepared to visit this planet. Maybe some smarter ones said, "No, thank you! I am good here. I do not need to have a human experience on planet Earth."

It feels like there is a certain expectation for the world's population by whoever sent us here. To meet their quota, they have to balance the population. So whatever quantity is sent, others are called back proportionately. Of course, they are not always sending ones who can actually shift the paradigm. At least not many of them. When the darkness and the light finally confirmed the battlefield for playing the game of life, the planet Earth was the obvious choice. They each had their wish list.

1. Both parties would have access to all of humans, regardless their gender, race, beliefs, or orientation. Absolutely no discrimination against anyone would be allowed.

2. Both parties would get fair opportunities to recruit players for their teams.

Well, when they realized the game is pretty boring, they wanted to spice it up a little bit by creating either chaos or miracles. However, for them to accomplish their goals, they need players who are above average, along with a few very special ones.

You can imagine the special ones do not just happen to fall out of a tree. They need to be built and harvested. They need to be engineered and put through tests before being sent to their temporary home called Earth. When someone is so special, both sides fight over that person. After all, that person is undoubtedly capable of either manifesting chaos or creating miracles.

Then what is the purpose of the inaccessible routes?

Have you ever noticed how some people seem to skip through daisies daily but still complain about the things that make you feel nauseated, once you hear them? Yes, they are the average ones. They will be given opportunities to have challenges based on their capacity. They are not interested in waking up because they don't even know they are sleepwalking. They will perform being a human, and, when their time is up, they will go back.

Some lives, on the other hand, are more challenging. When those people trip, not only do they break their front teeth, but they get sued for tripping on someone's perfectly manicured front lawn. On top of that, they also get stuck paying the dentist's bill. You probably know people like this.

Some will actually get on those routes where they do not find anything worthwhile and will give up before they reach the end. So, when they are offered another route, they will say, "No!" These are the ones who have the chance to earn extra credit during their assignment on Earth, but they choose not to take it.

Some will actually continue on that route to oblivion. However, these individuals will question, try to figure out, and, hopefully, examine the path they are on.

So, even though it may seem like some routes are challenging and some bridges take you nowhere, you still need to continue, if you can handle your special journey on Earth as a human being, because **there is nothing for nothing**.

The important thing is not just being able to survive the challenges. It is what you *do* with that experience. Did you learn from it? Are you going to go back to sleep afterwards? Or sharing it with others? Are you going to forget about it?

Which team do you want to be on?

When life's experiences take you to situations that are difficult to understand and introduce you to people who are challenging to be around, and when they offer you multiple choices, what are you going to do?

Here is a tip: Not everyone goes through this with their eyes open. Not everyone tries to gain wisdom through their suffering. Not everyone accepts that they are sleepwalking. So, if you find yourself on a challenging route, why do you think that is?

47

SUAVE POMPOUS

HOW WELL DO YOU think you know yourself? What if your idea of "the self" has another side that resides in your subconscious mind? How can you tell which one of the characters of "the self" is running the show?

We wear a suit magnificently engineered to adapt itself to anything in order to survive. It seems like most humans have the instinct to survive and also to be protected by someone or something that possesses unearthly powers. Through this, it becomes convenient to believe that while we will do our part to survive, in case we face a challenge, we will also receive help. It is a comforting thought, is it not?

It is just like learning to ride a bike for the first time. You are eager to do it yourself but keep checking behind you to make sure your parents are still there, in case you fall. It is as if we were given a certificate of lifetime support before arriving on this planet. Somehow, in our hearts, we believe we will be rescued even if our faith is kidnapped, that we will be visited when we are lonely and given a hand to pull ourselves up, when we fall down.

That certificate does not exist. You have probably wasted a lot of time waiting to be understood. Most likely, you have watched your life pass you by but felt stuck in the streets of your disappointment. You have waited and waited, but nobody has come to your rescue. Seasons have come and gone, but spring never visited your garden.

The suit you wear is your skin. It can be damaged by the elements of life. The more your skin is exposed to challenges, the better chance it has to become tougher and thicker. Even then, nothing can damage your skin as badly as your own dysfunctional thoughts about yourself. Your anger can burn it. Your harsh words can cut it. Your heartache can shrink it. No matter how many tattoos you apply to it, your skin still cannot cover every dysfunctional belief you create, so long as you continue to believe that, somehow, some things did not go your way.

So, your skin generates extra layer, and your mind makes sure you get the message. This is when your brand new alliance arrives to your existence. Your body will be your joint residence, but you won't share the same thoughts. Because the mind is a master puppeteer, it will not be overwhelmed by the orchestration of your different characters. On the contrary, your mind will get a kick out of it.

Imagine being isolated not because of your personality, but simply because of your sense of fashion. How many of us actually think the reason we are not invited to a cool gathering has anything to do with our sense of fashion? Instead, we take it to the core. Does my mouth smell? Am I not cool enough? Is it my name? Is it my accent? Oh no! Could it be my freckles? Maybe my hair... Maybe this... or maybe that...

Have we not felt or thought this way at some point in our lives? **We are programmed to internalize things first**, so we act like we are satisfied with what are served. When we do that, we are not true to ourselves and another version of "the self" steps into the picture, saying, "Listen! If you are not going to tell them, then I will."

Unfortunately, not every character of the self helps to support your wellbeing. You may sabotage yourself. You may destroy your own bridges. You may block your own rivers and dry your own lakes. How would you feel if you were borrowing from your own happiness but doing nothing to pay it back? When you reach a point of no return and feel like you have exhausted all your resources, when you cannot collect your broken pieces, what are you going to do? **Darkness is flirtatious.** It will use its suave nature to hide its pompousness. You will smell its fragrant scent, but you will not notice its poisonous petals. You will pet its puppy face, but you will overlook its razor fangs.

Darkness will not reveal everything to you at once. Yes, it can take sides with your idea of the self. For example, we get confused about the value of pride and whether it is good for our confidence or bad for our compassion. Pride can be good to a certain point, but the distance between that point, where you stand, and the person you will annoy is less than a hair's breadth. It only takes a second for them to isolate you. If pride craves pomposity, you better know that you, too, will fall, and your pride will suffer. This could be a good thing, however, as it can teach you to be more humble and more compassionate.

Anything you possess that you believe is of good quality may not be of similar value to someone else around you. However, this is not to say that you have to alter yourself for those around you. For the most part, **the journey of self-recognition and acceptance is experienced on isolated roads.** If you want to meet your true self, do not waste your time looking for yourself in public places or in someone else's eyes. Your journey is your own, but it does not mean it always has to be traveled alone.

You just need to be careful about who accompanies you on your road to discovering yourself. Just as you may encounter the suave pompous, you may also come across truly genuine, compassionate beings who travel with stinging butterflies, cute, rabid bunnies, innocent anacondas, dieting vampires, nurturing assassins, and many employees of the darkness who are willing to do every sort of gymnastics to persuade you. So do not be so ignorant as to think such things will never happen to you. The question is how are you going to recognize who truly is whom and what is truly what? **Your inner compass can guide you correctly only if your**

alignment is right with yourself. Imagine if your true north actually resides in the south. Just think about it.

For someone who thinks it is okay to drive while be drunk, their north is their south. For someone who thinks it is okay to steal, their west is their east.

How can you rely on your compass if your senses are all tangled up? How can you find your way when everywhere feels dark?

Darkness does not have to be your enemy. Some of us even adapt comfortably to lives in the darkness. The darkness starts to provide for us. It starts to feed our dramas with chocolate cake and ice cream. Once we become familiar with its kitchen, we start to help ourselves to its goods. But we do not pay attention to the maggots dancing in our dessert.

Making a stupid mistake is similar to eating a dessert topped with maggots. Even if you can digest it, others around you might experience a stomach ache or nausea just watching you go through it.

When you fall into the well of the darkness, you will not have the luxury of slowing your fall. It happens very quickly. One minute, you are in a meadow of your dreams, skipping through daisies, and the next minute you take a wrong step and fall into the well. It is very likely you were too busy being in your head and did not notice the warning sign. Instead of going through the hassle of putting up a warning sign that can easily be missed among the overgrown grass of our ignorant minds, you might be thinking why isn't that hazardous well sealed shut in the first place.

Are you saying the employees of the darkness should not have a job?

That is what their job is all about. They are not going to cover the holes or wells. They are not going to make the light switches easily accessible. They are not going to give up because you are intelligent. In fact, they get a promotion when they trick a smart one into making a stupid mistake. It is easy for the darkness to trick those who are sleepwalking. But those who are mindful can also be tricked. They, too, can fall. And when they fall, the sound of their pride hitting bottom can be heard in faraway places.

Try to imagine the act of falling like this:

The fall is like throwing a rock into very calm water. It alters the smooth surface of the water by creating ripples on first contact.

The water is your environment: your family, your friends, and the universe.

Your identity is the rock.

The mistake you make is created by your stupidity.

Your stupidity is the hand that threw the rock into the water.

The effects of your mistake are the ripples on the water.

If you think, once the rock sinks all the way to the bottom and it naturally disappears, the ripples will stop vibrating after awhile, and all observers on the shore will eventually leave, as well... Well... not quite.

First of all, everyone will take a picture of that rock from every possible angle. Then, the photos will be published everywhere, so anybody who wants to feel good about themselves can compare their self-proclaimed grace to your unforgivable stupidity. They will not so easily forget about that rock. And since your mistake caused discomfort in their sight, you may not be forgiven by them, either.

The ripples are going to create a reaction in whoever was connected to you. And those ripples will reach to the shore.

Meanwhile, your self-image will struggle all the way down to the bottom, where it is dark and cold. What if your identity never recovers? Is this how your self-image dies?

What happens to the person who actually threw your identity into the dark, cold bottom of the water?

The bottom of the water is now your new residence. It is called "humility." Welcome!

Now what?

Clearly, there is no light at the bottom of the water. And, in the dark, you think you cannot see.

However, we can adjust our vision to see in the dark. But this can take time. You cannot rush it. The best thing to do at that time is accept the fact that your "self" is now at the bottom. You know how it feels if you have fallen. Unfortunately, most of us interpret the message incorrectly, and we try to save the rock. We think we can redeem ourselves if only we can get that rock back to the shore.

Remember, the rock is the identity; the "self" image. Identity, however, is an experience that is not permanent at all. This is an excellent opportunity to leave your false "self" identity at the bottom of the lake.

Let it go.

You actually have never left the shore. In fact, you were awake and conscious when you threw your identity. This is the part of healing where you start to see your true self by letting the "identity" you have been holding onto disappear. That is the moment when you say goodbye to "suave pomposity."

When you are ready to move on, you will notice some people still talking about the ripples, even when the surface of the water is already calm. Some people make their dull lives more interesting by talking about the ripples of others but fail to look at the ocean of their ignorance. In that ocean, where waves carry their curiosity and reasoning from one empty shore to another empty shore, they spend their entire lives lingering between the islands of their own stories. They make their screenplay their one-and-only reality.

Then isn't it better to hit bottom, if it is going to wake you up? Or would you rather dance with the characters you have created on the pages of your story based on your neverending drama?

Wake up! Go to the shore of your awakening. Kiss goodbye your identity and throw it out to sea. You will see that your so-called identity is nothing but an extra layer of skin that can be damaged by the elements of life. You can either wait until it consumes you or you can take off that extra layer and see your true skin, which exists underneath.

48

LEAVING HOME

"**HOW WAS CLASS** today?" his guardian asked.

"It was really intriguing. The elder one talked about a very spacial place called Earth. Do you know anything about this location?" he wanted to know.

His guardian remained silent for a minute. He appeared next to his novice and asked, "Yes, I do. I was there once, on an assignment."

"How was it? Can you tell me?"

"It is not my place to answer that. Why are you interested in the Earth so much?"

"Because the elder one told us about the internship. And I am intrigued by it."

"Have you signed up for it?"

"Yes! We will go there to collect data and return once the mission is over."

"So, when are you going to have your interview then?"

"Tomorrow."

The guardian left after talking with his novice. Some thoughts danced around his head, but he chose not to dance with them tonight.

In the morning, while in the class, those who had signed up to have their internship on Earth were asked to leave the class. Then they were taken to the place where the interviews would be held.

Each novice received the exact same information. They all got their to-do list before taking off. However, the elder one approached the novice and told him he needed to wait, as his guardian wanted to share something. So the elder one left the room to meet with the guardian.

"I am sure you know this already," the guardian told the elder.

"Yes, I know he is very special," the elder replied.

"We have to make sure he remembers us."

"We cannot interfere. You know that. Just like we could not interfere with you and your other version. You came back here and did not go to the other side. If your novice awakens, then he, too, will come back here."

"Can I least give him a little reminder?"

"Yes," the elder one replied. He then went back in the room with the guardian.

The novice was waiting. The guardian looked at his novice and asked, "What will you remember most about your home?"

"I don't know."

"Do you know what the darkness is?"

"I don't know."

"The darkness is something you will never see here. We are the light."

"We are?"

"Here. Take this. Before you become a human, I want you to have this." He then pointed at his novice's heart and put something inside. "You will need this," he said. "If you ever get lost, I want you to listen to it."

"What is it?"

"It is the music of your heart. May you never lose it."

"I remember you telling me you also were there once."

The guardian then looked at the elder. He knew he was not allowed to reveal anything else.

The elder approached the novice and said, "When you start your human life, your other version also starts his human life."

"What? I don't understand. What do you mean my other version?"

"**Each one of you has the potential to choose either the darkness or the light**," the elder replied.

"But why am I already here then, in the light?"

"Because we all are light. We always send the light beings to the Earth. During your journey over there, you will be in the river of oblivion. Once you leave here, the darkness will be after you. They cannot come here. However, on planet Earth, the darkness can survive. They will certainly try to recruit you. More than once."

"Did they try to recruit my guardian, too?"

"Yes, but they could not succeed. That is why your guardian is here. The darkness will recognize your light when you are in the current of the river. They will chase you."

"What will I do? What if they take me? What if I never come back here again?"

"You belong to the light. For them to take you, they will have to gather all of their forces."

"What if they do?"

"Just remember the music of your heart. It will play your truth. Just listen to it."

# # #

The darkness will not miss an opportunity to recruit any human being. It will push you to your limits. During your journey to Earth, you will download a lot of data. You will be assigned to your chosen parents. Some of us jump out of the river of oblivion before our anticipated travel time. Some of us decide to go back. Upon arrival, the light will welcome you with love. You will remember love.

Then the next part of your journey will start. That journey is your assignment. You will go there to collect data. You need to have multiple experiences. Some of them will make you feel lighter, and some of them will make you feel like your life is not worth moving on.

Every challenge is designed and resolved by you and your other version. You will dance with yourself. In every challenge, there will be a choice. Depending on what you choose, one of you will lead that dance. There will be an audience from both sides. **Every decision will create a path**. Every path will come with an experience. Every experience will come with multiple scenarios and various outcomes. Nothing will actually end. It will transform into something else. You can only leave your lifeless body behind, nothing else. Your energy will travel. When your data has been collected, your assignment will be over, and you will come back home.

The river of oblivion is open to many beings, and not every one of them will come to this life as a human being. Some of them can be seen, and some of them are the unseen.

49

IN THE HOUSE OF REPENTANCE

SHE FELT HER heart's heaviness in her hand as she tried to hold the brush to paint her sorrow. She dipped the brush in the darker shade of her state of being. Tears fell from the brush and splashed her hope all over the ground, like the blood of her existence at a murder scene.

She believed sadness could kill one's hopes and dreams, so she struggled on the bridge of life and death. Her feet felt crushed under the burden of her guilt. Her cold fingers could not grasp what was happening. There was an emptiness in her eyes but not as big as the one in her heart. She believed nothing was big enough to fill the emptiness in her heart. Sadness was its only occupant, and nothing else could get in.

She started to paint the walls of her insecurity over the colors of summer that once were there. Her autumn had arrived too soon for her to bear. With the changing color of the leaves, she could not help but fall on the ground and wait for her winter. She believed the snow would cover her guilt and perhaps her heart would just stay there, frozen. Nobody would look for her anyway, because she thought her suffering could never be shared. Who would want to share someone else's suffering, anyway?

Her tears kept falling into the paint, making it a prosaic shade of gray. Although she closed her eyes to sleep, the emptiness still was there. Can anyone truly sleep through their sadness, even if their cradle is made out of air? Can anyone hear the music in their heart over the loud, neverending symphony of their guilt?

Her guilt felt too heavy to lift. She kept pacing up and down the corridors of her regret. If she could reverse her mistake or eliminate that moment as if it had never happened, she knew she would do that in a heartbeat. If she knew everyone who had been hurt by the mistake she had made, she would be knocking on their doors to beg them for forgiveness. However, would anyone open their door to someone who had fallen from grace?

She allowed her tired body to sink into the couch. She could barely keep alive her thinning instinct to fight for herself. With no energy to contemplate one more time where she had gone wrong, she could not resist the need of her wounded body to collapse. She involuntarily fell into sleep on her bed of nightmares in the house of repentance.

The darkness was her guide at the time when she made her biggest mistake. Since then, she knew the darkness was still leading her game. Because her prayers felt ignored, she thought they would never be answered. Even then, she could at least entertain the idea of her prayers being received. But just like some of us believe in cause and effect, she, too, believed, if she found the courage to pray for help, then help should have been sent to her long ago. She should not have been abandoned in the forever-lasting winters of her suffering.

# # #

The law of life works independent from your version of cause and effect. Sometimes, the results are apparent immediately, but sometimes the results get stuck at the gates of customs. Perhaps we are not in control of everything in our lives. Maybe you cannot control the time and its teaching curriculum. If you want to be in its classroom, perhaps then you need to stick to its schedule. So, although karma may seem to be running late according to your calculations, perhaps it is not late at all.

While she feels like she has been abandoned in the forever-lasting winter of her suffering, neither the darkness nor the light gives up on her. Remember, they both are experts and they are both persuasive.

Those who know the taste of suffering will not visit the same shade of the darkness as you do. However, when you are in the dark, does it really matter if you compare your darkness to others? No, not at all. However, **falling into the darkness comes with many opportunities for those who are willing to grab them**. But if you are stuck in your own self-pity, then you likely will miss the point. There is light in the darkness. However, you need to be awake and mindful to see it.

For some, falling into the darkness is just like falling into quicksand or a whirlpool in the ocean of your confusion. For some, it is like tasting a sour grape. Maybe your type of darkness means nothing to another. None of this matter. This is not a competition to prove who suffers the most.

If you have enough time to compare your darkness to others', then use that time to understand where you really are. When you are in the house of repentance, it feels like you have left the windows open during a stubborn blizzard. It takes all your strength to get up and close the windows. You look around to find something to keep you warm. In that moment of thinking, the darkness will steal your firewood.

Your hope is the firewood.

The blizzard is the process of going back into society, not knowing whether you will be accepted in.

Your fire is your breath and your heartbeat. If you want to live, you have to have the fire.

You could be the type of individual who, during his suffering, actually considers leaving the windows open, and who does not really want to start the fire. If you are that individual, do not be ashamed of your state of being at that moment of fatigue. It takes courage to look at the beast in the eye. It takes power to swim back to the shore. And only you will know how it feels to fight with sharks and the other monsters of the ocean.

If you truly believe there is no hope, not only will the darkness will steal your firewood, but it will also remove anything flammable in your environment, so you can never start your fire. It will eliminate the trees from your forest. It will take you back and drop you right in the middle of your ocean. You will know by then that there is no life in the water for any type of fire. So, can you truly afford to have no hope? Why would you even be in the house of repentance? Why not the house of ignorance?

Sometimes, all you need is a little spark. If the darkness can steal your fire, you must know that the light will give you an opportunity to find your spark again.

While you are lost in your lamentation, because your self-pity has destroyed all the signs, for a split second your eyes might glance outside your window. Even if it seems almost impossible to see anything in the snowstorm of your own doing, you might actually see someone out there. You will first question your sanity, wondering whether there really was someone out there or whether what you saw was a ghost. You will cover your eyes like a little kid, hoping that, when you open them, that person will no longer be standing there. You will even count, "one-Mississippi, two-Mississippi…"

However, among the howls of the wind, between the razor-edged snowflakes, next to igloos built by wolves, and just on the cracked surface of a frozen lake, you will notice that that person is still waiting. You would come closer to the window, forgetting for that moment the shackles of your fear. In that very same moment, you will take a leap of faith in order to see who that person might be. This curiosity to think about someone else's wellbeing is your spark. It is your hope.

When you realize the person out there is not going anywhere, you will decide to go out and ask if she needs anything. However, the second you step outside, she will turn around and step off the cracks in the frozen lake. You will raise your voice, hoping she can hear you. She will continue to walk, and you will start to follow her by stepping on the same cracks in the frozen lake. It feels like you could fall into the chilling reality of your failures, but you continue to walk, instead. You can see her next to the wolves. She looks at you and then at the wolves next to her. You will recognize the feeling of familiarity but won't remember from where and how. After she leaves, you will arrive at the igloo. The wolf will come to you as if he wants to welcome an old friend. The razor-edged snowflakes will now be soft and will melt as the howls of the wind turn into a lullaby.

The lullaby wil sound familiar, and you will no longer feel the cold. While she waits for you on the bridge, your heaviness will lift. You will go to her, but this time she will not move. She will wait for you.

You will draw closer to her and feel goosebumps on your skin when you notice she is identical to you. Between reality and a dreamlike state, she will tell you about the bridge of choices.

She wants you to look at all the ships on the water. You want to know about one of them but then realize that ship is the one that never brings its passengers back. She will tell you that you won't be on it ,as you have made a choice to follow her, instead. She then will tell you about the other ships. Before she disappears, she will look at you and say, "Did you like the lullaby?"

"Yes. How did you know about it?"

"Because I once told you about the music in your heart. You were my assignment tonight."

50

ABSTRUSE ASSIGNMENTS

SOMETIMES, WE END UP in the city of perplexity while on our way to reaching the pot at the end of a rainbow. All we can say is, *"What happened?"*

Honestly, how did we end up there? Yes, while it is true that not every road is clear and the signs are often difficult to see because they are not well lit, this does not make it any easier to get over our disbelief. Did we miss the exit? Did someone actually hide the sign? Did I doze off? Is this map old? Did I write down the directions incorrectly?

And some of us, after allowing our minds to find a reason for our unplanned detour, actually decide to go with the flow and explore the city of perplexity. Then we postpone our meeting with the leprechaun at the end of a rainbow until the time is right.

Could there be a reason for taking detours or getting lost? Is the universal director of the movie we are acting in sitting on his chair, saying, "Cut! You know what? Change this scene. It is too predictable. The audience is expecting them to find the pot. Let's make this more interesting. Let's create a detour. This is so much more fun. Okay. Get ready. And… *Action!*"

Then it almost feels like we should be given a reward for finding our way because, when we get lost, it seems we become the fool of the village. We also then become the main course at all the gossip-sponsored dinner parties.

When we are lost, we know we can no longer recognize our environment. That is not really difficult. But how do we recognize being lost in our existence? Do we have a system set up for ourselves that tells us, "You now are officially lost. You will now start going through such and such steps for exactly twenty-one days. Take notes and listen to your assignment carefully. Then it will be over. You will surely find yourself again."

You only wish it were that easy. Some people don't even know they are lost. Also, while decoding your assignment that you didn't even know you had, have you ever received such clear instructions, supported by a full-time expert?

So why can't we get lessons that can be learned easily? Why do we have to climb up the highest mountain only to find that what we were looking for is actually in the apartment of our downstairs neighbor? Why do we have to study and practice a particular belief to find faith, but then lose it as if it was dust in the wind? Why do we fall in love but then fall out of it?

Can we not just get some warning in advance, instead of experience regret lectured by a professor of humility? Why do we have such confusing assignments to complete, yet we can only access such small portions of our brain capacity?

Perhaps there is not just one director for the movie we are playing in. Does it not feel like sometimes we are guided brilliantly on the runway by eternal lights, but then sometimes we don't even get even a hint and find ourselves tripping over a penny because somebody has glued it to the pavement?

We are told "how to be good" in cleverly inserted ways, but we are overlooked when it comes to finding our way back, when we are lost.

If two directors are working on the same movie, who is going to pay for their dispute? The actors?

Now, coming back to our reality, one should perhaps think about creating our own life's map. If there is a supposed connection between the stars, if there is a history of each continent and of the oceans in between, if there is an order among the planets, then shouldn't our lives also have some coordinates? Should we not be able to write down some significant events of our lives and see how far they can be traced back? What about someone you met in kindergarten who comes back into your life after many years? Why is that?

How about getting the detour in our lives? Not the one where you say, "Oh, well. We'll just turn around. Not a big deal." But the one where you have to say, "Oh no! I am dead. There is no way I can get out of this. That's it! My life is officially over."

R.I.P. It was a very difficult assignment. He could not decode it. So is that it? Every time we get lost, should we just give up because of the abstruse assignment?

When what you go through seems too perplexing, do not close the book and put it away. It is a hurdle, a math question, and anything that will push your boundaries. Nothing is permanent, so neither are your boundaries and limitations. **The more comfortable you get, the less free your imagination will be**.

These assignments will only be given to those who make a commitment to learn from them and share their wisdom they experience through suffering while translating the clues in their assignments. However, your assignment will never come with a cheat-sheet.

Just like when anything comes into our lives easily, we may certainly appreciate and be thankful for it, but we may not necessarily analyze its journey from wherever it started to the moment it landed in our laps.

When something is earned, it creates a bond so we will remember the value of the sweat and tears we put into it. Just like witnessing someone else's fall will not bruise your knees, copying someone else's awakening will not make you enlightened.

Yes, your assignments, whether they are as simple as being happy or as complicated as life itself, are worth working on. When you get stuck, believe it or not, you will get support.

But you have to do your part first.

That is making a commitment to being true. In fact, that is how everything else unfolds.

Be true.

You will see.

ACKNOWLEDGMENTS

I **WOULD LIKE** to extend my sincere thanks to these incredible individuals and organizations listed below, for their parts in manifesting this book. I am aware of the fact that no story can ever fully be about its writer or teller. I am almost certain I have forgotten to include some wonderful people here. For that reason, please do accept my heartfelt apologies, as it was not intentional. This book does exist because of every being I have encountered in my life, regardless if they were visible to the eye or not.

My beautiful daughters Olivia, Eden, and Ava, my teachers, my wonderful family, my editor Kathryn F. Galán at Wynnpix Productions, all the monks at the Atammayatarama Buddhist Monastery and the Sangha, Sue Adams & Kevin Ross, Levent Akbag, Aydan & Zihni Akca, Nesrin Akoren, Connie and Nat Balloo, Marti Charbonneau, Ven. Santidhammo Bhikku, Ann Childers, Carolyn Croshaw, , Bhante Dewananda, Dharma Buddies, Eric Dowsett, Jennifer Eby, Catherine Freeman & Tim Oldfield, Andrew Freeman, Roberta Giffin, Mine Hakim, RayAnne Harter, Elcin Hasgul, Tracey Hepner, Sirin Hepcorman, Dolores Holt, Paul Hopkins, Cindy & Jim Johnson, Nevin Kademlioglu, Zeki Karabilgin, Saniye Kaufhold, Phaedra Kelly, Shannon Kelly, Kay Kennedy, Michael Ismail Kilic, Kimberly Kingsley, Laura Kovacs, Decker Lang, Cigdem Lilley, Pete Lindahl, David Marshall, Jim Matthews, Carole & Harry McCarthy, Debbie McKenzie, Megan Meade, Brian Minsk, Mary Moore, Nilhan Sayin Oner, Sunantha Ouk, Harold Palmer, Cindy Peart-Davis,

Paula Pedroso, Pranee Poyns, Fabio Refosco, Michele Rimmele, Sonam Rinpoche, **Reuel Robertson,** Gavin Rushevics, **Mary Salsberry,** Amanda & Omer Sam, **Ulker Sezer,** Bev & Don Schmidt, Kathy Schramm, Kristina Selset, **Meltem Duzgider Sipahi,** Elisabeth De Amaral Sorvik, Eveay Tatman, Ritthi Thirajitto, Maureen Tracy, Max Warren, Jay Williamson, Faith Wilson, Sheri Zocco.

ABOUT AYHAN

AYHAN YAVUZ is a writer and artist who lives in Bothell, Washington. *Azra's Labyrinth* is his first novel and the first in *The Realm of Illusions* series. *In the Cradle of Umbra,* about becoming more aware of life's lessons, understanding the anatomy of an opportunity called *suffering,* and the quest for acceptance and happiness, is his first book of non-fiction.

Ayhan was born in Turkey, studied in England, and currently lives in the United States. Before becoming the artist and the author he is now, Ayhan spent several years in the financial industry, worked as a counselor, studied multiple holistic healing modalities, and also became ordained as a Buddhist Monk at the Atammayatarama Buddhist Monastery in Woodinville, Washington, where he continues to practice Buddhism and learn to become more mindful with gratitude and humility. He is committed to peace, truth, and giving back to any he can help.

Find more about him at www.tresoea.com.

Made in the USA
Columbia, SC
10 January 2025

51581720R00140